Elephants Have the Right of Way

Toro Girls School—air view.

Elephants Have the Right of Way

Dr. William D. Stewart

VANTAGE PRESS
New York

FIRST EDITION

All rights reserved, including the right of
reproduction in whole or in part in any form.

Copyright © 2010 by William D. Stewart

Manufactured by Vantage Press, Inc.
419 Park Ave. South, New York, NY 10016

Printed in the United States of America
ISBN: 978-0-533-16273-4

Library of Congress Catalog Card No: 2009906590

0 9 8 7 6 5 4 3 2 1

Uganda is a fairy tale. You climb up a railway instead of a beanstalk, and at the end there is a wonderful new world. The scenery is different, and, most of all, the people are different from anything elsewhere to be seen in the whole range of Africa.

—Winston Churchill
My African Journey (1908)

Elephants Have the Right of Way

1

Everyone was sad. It was because of our dog, Vicky. Nobody would take her. Relatives, friends, neighbors—nobody wanted that dog. We packed the car with the kids, luggage, toys, books, lunch, and the dog. I can't take the dog to Africa. When I stopped for gas, everyone had to use the bathroom. Mother was with four children in the bathroom while I was alone with Vicky and the gas station attendant. Then he said it. "Nice dog you got there." "Yes," I replied, "great dog! Everyone should have a dog. It develops character and teaches responsibility to children. Do you have a dog?" "Well," he said, "I used to have a dog, but it got hit by a car. Right here at the station. I was pumping gas, the dog ran out after a car, and that was that. Dead as a politician's promise."

I had to work fast. The kids would be returning to the car soon, and I had to get rid of that dog before they got back. "You know, that's a fine dog. She doesn't chase cars, is housebroken, has had all her shots, and is spayed. I've got to get rid of that dog because we are moving to Africa and can't take the dog. I would be obliged to you if you would take this dog. Her name is 'Vicky,' and I know you'll give her a good home. Now, listen, the kids are in the bathroom and they'll be coming out soon. So, why don't you take Vicky back in your office before they get back to the car? I'll give you ten dollars for her first bag of dog food." I put a ten-dollar bill in his hand, opened the door of the car, and gave him Vicky's leash. The man seemed pleased with either the dog or the ten dollars. I was not sure which, but, the dog was gone. As Vicky was led back to the attendant's office, a sweeping feeling of sadness came over me.

Everybody jumped back into the car. "I want the window seat." "No, it's my turn for the window." "You're sitting on my book." "Where's my doll?" This confusion went on while I drove away from the gas station. We stopped for a red light and Stephen said, "Where's the dog? We've left Vicky. Where's Vicky?" Now everyone started looking around the car and yelling, "The dog!" "The dog!" "We've lost the dog." "We've lost Vicky!" "Turn around! "Stop the car!" "We have to go back and find Vicky!" "DADDDD!!!!"

This was going to take some diplomacy. What do I tell the kids about the dog? "I gave your dog to the gas station man." No, that wouldn't cut it. Try the "Aren't we nice to be so kind to that poor man" appeal. "Well, kids, I was talking to the gas station man, and he told me that his dog got run over by a car. He looked so sad. He saw Vicky and said that she looked just like his poor dog. He was petting Vicky, and she was wagging her tail and licking his hand. I felt sorry for him. He said he wished he had a dog like Vicky to take the place of the dog that he lost. So, I thought that we could let him take care of Vicky while we are in Africa. When we get back home, we can stop and get Vicky back again." The kids were crying, but I could see that it was working. The children had been told that we would not be able to take Vicky to Africa, and they knew that she had to go to someone. The sobbing was replaced with conversation about Africa and what we would do there and our first ride in an airplane. Vicky was forgotten for the moment. Everyone was thinking about the airplane, Newark Airport, New York City, and Africa. Africa! Elephants, lions, hippos, giraffe.

It was the first week in May that I had seen the ad in the Sunday edition of the *New York Times.* "Teach Business Subjects in East Africa." I was reading the "Week in Review" section of the *Times* at the kitchen table. Smiling, I said to my wife, Joyce, "Let's go to Africa. The University of Massachusetts is advertising a teaching job in their 'Uganda Project' in East Africa." It sounded good to me, but Joyce wasn't interested. "I'm happy just where I am. You go, I'll stay here with the kids."

Joyce felt "secure" in Alfred. We had not had an easy time while I was going to college with a family of four children, "Bill." Joyce said, "We've just started to get established here at Alfred. You can't leave your job and go traipsing off across the world with a family. The kids are doing well in school and John is looking forward to going to school next year. You can't stay in Africa the rest of your life. What will you do for a job when Africa is over?"

"This ad says 'two years,' " I replied. "If SUNY would give me a two-year leave, we could have two years of travel. It would be like a vacation after the years we spent in college."

College had been full-time, including summer schools for me. During this time, I had also worked at a variety of jobs—Sears Roebuck, clerking in a pharmacy, and even selling roofing and siding.

For Joyce the college years had been spent working as a registered nurse and having babies. The babies just kept coming, and coming, and coming, and coming. This was before the days of "The Pill."

I had been at SUNY Alfred for the past three years. We were not able to save a lot of money, but we were paying our bills. The college loans were just about paid, and we had started a modest savings account for a down payment on a home. Now, Joyce was a full-time mother and homemaker. We were located close to family and friends, and had "settled into" a pleasant and predictable life. The children liked having their friends, their school, their room, and their dog. I should have been happy at Alfred, but I wanted more. I didn't know "what" I wanted; but I wanted something more. Africa would be "more."

"Joyce," I said, "now is the time to go to Africa. The children haven't established friends as they will when they're older and we're not tied down to a house. In a few years Africa would be out of the question. Now it is possible."

I read through the ad again, "Teach business subjects in Africa." I got the scissors, cut out the ad, and started to rough draft a letter to Elwyn Doubleday at the University of Massachusetts in Amherst.

We could never go to Africa. No one was going to send a man with a wife and four young children to Africa. It was just something to talk about. "Hey, kids," I said, "let's go to Africa to see the elephants, the lions, the giraffe." The girls were ready to go. "Yea, Africa! The elephants, the lions." Stephen wasn't excited about that prospect. He was taking a cue from mother, who was not interested in going anywhere. John was three, and three didn't understand Africa. The only elephants and lions John was familiar with were the ones that he had seen in his books. *Horton Hatches the Egg* was about as familiar as he was with elephants. It was just fun to talk about. Then Elywn Doubleday called and said he would like to pay us a visit.

I arrived home from school and told Joyce, "I got a call today from Elwyn Doubleday." "Who is Elwyn Doubleday?" she asked. "You remember, that Elwyn Doubleday from the University of Massachusetts and the

African thing, that 'Uganda Project'. The guy I wrote the letter to." Joyce was not happy. "I'm not going to Africa." "Well," I said, "Elwyn Doubleday is going to be here next week and talk to us about Africa."

For the next week I read everything in the college library I could find about Uganda. Africa! A man is coming to my home from the University of Massachusetts to talk with me about going to Africa. All I thought about was Africa, Uganda, and traveling. How many people did I know who had taken a family and moved across the world? No one. Is this crazy or what? I didn't think I would be sent to Africa, but I wanted to. This would be "more."

The telephone rang while we were doing dishes after dinner. Joyce washed, the kids dried, and I put things away. "Hello," I said. "Hello, this is Elwyn Doubleday. I plan on driving out to see you tomorrow. How long a trip is Alfred, New York from Amherst, Massachusetts?" I put my hand over the telephone and said, "Joyce, it's Elwyn Doubleday. He's going to be here tomorrow. How long a trip is Alfred, New York from Amherst, Massachusetts?" I put my hand over the telephone and said, "Joyce, it's Elwyn Doubleday. He's going to be here tomorrow." I gave Elwyn the directions to my home and said "Goodbye." Joyce was not looking forward to going to Africa or even talking to Doubleday about it.

I was thinking about what we would gain by going to Africa, Joyce was thinking about what we would lose. She would lose her parents, her church, and her friends. The kids were going to lose grandma and grampa, their school, their rooms, and Vicky.

As I watched the car coming down our driveway, I knew it must be Elwyn Doubleday. At that point it was as though I were seeing our situation for the first time. I wondered what the Doubledays thought of our home.

Our house seemed to be "hanging" on the side of a steep embankment. The driveway started a quarter-mile to the north and edged up the hillside until it reached the small, flat spot the house was built on. The house was constructed of cement block with a red tile roof. In front of the house was a small yard, the embankment covered with thorn bush, the road, a swamp, the railroad tracks, and woods. There were no other houses visible in any direction. In back of the house and up the hill, was the skeleton of what must have been a large chicken coop at one time. Directly behind the house, along the driveway, was a dilapidated building that served as a garage. I wished I had gone to U. Mass for this interview.

In Uganda a year later, I asked Elwyn, "Didn't you feel guilty sending American families to the African jungles?" "I felt guilty about everyone but you and Williams." Elwyn replied, "Tororo is a step up from Alfred or Apache Junction, Arizona. For you two it was an improvement in living conditions."

Elwyn Doubleday is a down-home, soft-spoken man with an assuring smile that encourages confidence. "So, you're the man who wants to go to Uganda," Elwyn said as he got out of his car. "This is my wife, Peg." Turning to my wife, I said, "And this is Joyce and our youngest child, John." John was a bit shy and wrapped his arms around his mother's leg. "The other three children are in school," Joyce said. I think she was hoping family size would discourage Elwyn from hiring me.

I liked Elwyn right away. He is easy going and easy to talk with. I could tell Joyce liked him also. Elwyn's wife, Peg, is a motherly type of woman who made their visit seem like a visit from relatives. We just felt comfortable with them. Nice people.

Elwyn had brought a slide projector with color slides

of Tororo Girls School, which was the "Uganda Project." As Elwyn set up the projector and screen, I drew the window curtains. We saw pictures of Tororo Girls School—dormitories, auditorium, cafeteria, administration and teaching blocks, and the faculty housing. "There are seven ranch-style houses for families," Elwyn explained. "This is the house you would be living in. It's right on the campus. The house and utilities are provided to you as part of your employment package. Your next-door neighbors are from Massachusetts on one side and from New York—down toward the city—on the other. There is also a family from Arizona and a woman from Washington, D.C. The people from Massachusetts and Arizona both have three children your children's ages. The people from New York have a two-year-old boy and a baby girl. So, your children would have American friends."

The job sounded "great" to me. I would be given a much larger salary than I was receiving at SUNY Alfred. In addition, I would not have to pay income taxes if I stayed out of the States for 18 months. At the end of the first year we were entitled to a month's vacation anywhere in Europe. While in Uganda we would be living, rent free, in a new ranch-style house with all utilities paid. My assignment in Uganda would be at a USAID funded, University of Massachusetts staffed school for African girls. The teaching duties would be essentially the same as those I had in the Secretarial Department at SUNY.

State University of New York agreed to give me a leave of absence, so I would be able to return to Alfred and my job at SUNY at the end of my two years in Uganda. Joyce finally said she would go after I promised her we would return to Alfred with enough for a down payment on our own home, and that I would "never, ever" ask her to leave the States again. I called Elwyn, and told him I would take the job. All that was left was the physicals, immunization shots, and passports.

The Typhoid-Paratyphoid immunizations were the worst. After the children had gotten these shots, they all vomited on the way home from the doctor's office. That night they were running 102-degree fevers, and the next day I was so sick I couldn't get out of bed. If that's the cure, what can the disease be like? What a list of immunizations! The yellow fever immunizations required a call to the CDC in Atlanta, Georgia. They did something to eggs and flew the resulting liquid in a frozen state to the hospital at Cornell University. Cornell University called us, and we had to drive to Ithaca that day to get the shots.

When we boarded the plane that would fly us from Binghamton, New York to Newark Airport, the afternoon sun was pouring through the plane's windows in yellow squares of light. People were finding spaces for luggage, locating the right seat, taking off coats, finding seat belts, and opening newspapers and magazines. The attendants were locating seats, and putting things away while they counted people, empty seats, and checked boarding pass numbers. Everyone was just about settled down and had their seat belts on. Stephen, Paula, Beth, and John had examined the ash trays, the shades that pull down on the windows, the little white air sick bags, and the buttons that adjust the seats. When the activity was over, when everyone was sitting in their seats, I saw Paula's eyes brimming with tears which were about to trickle down her cheeks in little rivers of sadness.

The airline stewardess also saw this and knelt down beside Paula's seat in the aisle and said, "Would you like some peanuts?" To which Paula said, "Thank you," and took the peanuts. The stewardess, pointing to Stephen, Beth, and John said, "Are these your brothers and sister?" Everyone smiled and said, "Yes." The stewardess smiled and said, "And you're all going to New York?" "No, we're going to Africa!" Stephen said. "Africa," replied the stewardess, "Oh, that will be wonderful; the elephants, the lions." "Oh, yes," everyone said, "the elephants, and the lions, and the giraffes, Africa!"

Newark Airport seemed big to us. We had stepped onto an airplane in a small, familiar place and stepped out into a great mass of people. All kinds of people. Men with turbans and long beards. Women with long colorful robes. Black people with strange hair which hung like ropes woven with gold and silver bands. Strange languages spoken in accents we had never heard before. We moved along in this great swell of humanity with four little children. What am I doing moving to Africa with four children ages eight, six, five, and three? There was no time to think of that. We were busy keeping track of tickets, passports, bathroom trips, and snacks. When you want to keep children busy, give them something they can do. Eat! Hot dogs, french fries, and soda.

At Newark we got on another and bigger airplane. Most of the people were black. As we looked out the windows, we could see the Statue of Liberty. "Look, kids," I said, "there's the Statue of Liberty!" "Where?" "What's the Statue of Liberty?" I have to go to the bathroom." That was John. He always had to go the bathroom. I don't think he had to "use" the bathroom, he just wanted to "see" the bathroom. We waited, and waited, and waited to take off. The people were getting restless. The plane was filled with smoke and the sounds of people talking and laughing. The children were squirming in their seats when we heard a voice from the intercom. "Ladies and gentlemen, since this flight is direct to Africa and is very long, the plane must carry a large quantity of fuel. This adds weight to the airplane and necessitates using the longest runway. Domestic planes have priority, and we will have to wait a while to get clearance. We should be taking off in less than an hour. In the meantime, the stewardess will be serving complimentary drinks of your choice. During this time you may leave your seat if you wish." If you want to keep children busy, feed them. If you want to keep adults busy, give them free drinks.

The stewardess came down the aisle giving the passengers little bottles of scotch, vodka, whiskey, gin, wine, soda, and packages of peanuts. At that point, the plane took on a different atmosphere. It was more like a cocktail lounge with people standing in the aisles drinking, smoking, eating peanuts, laughing and talking.

The afternoon light had gone. It was dark outside and the Statue of Liberty had been replaced by runway lights and the square, white lights of the airport terminal windows. The laughing had been replaced by complaints and grumbling. Somewhere a voice cried out "When are we going to get going?" "Let's get going!" Then there was a voice from the intercom. "Ladies and gentlemen, we are now clear for takeoff." There was a loud cheer from the passengers. "However," the intercom continued, "we have been idling so long that we no longer have sufficient fuel for the flight. We will have to go back to the terminal for fuel. I am sorry and thank you for you patience. Please bear with us. I have been assured that we will be given priority status for take off." The laughing stopped and was replaced by complaints. "OHHH, NO! What kind of a plane is this?" Groans. "I will never take this airline again!" "What terrible service." "What do you think this is; second-rate for Africa?" I also heard an occasional

"Shit!" and other such descriptive words expressing the passengers' feeling about the situation. Stephen leaned toward me, "Do we have to get off the airplane?" Paula and Beth were asking why we couldn't go and what happened. The plane was hot and smoked filled. The people had been given too much alcohol. Instead of being "pacified" by the alcohol, it had removed the passengers' inhibitions, and they were angry and complaining. We had been idling in an airplane for almost two hours with another eighteen hours to go.

After we finally took off, the overhead lights were turned off in the airplane's cabin. Most of the passengers were asleep. some passengers had seat lights on. These were the midnight readers, card players, and twos or threes quietly talking. The kids and Joyce were sleeping. My eyes were shut, and I could hear the gentle "WHOOSH" of the plane slipping through the night to Africa. A voice kept saying, "What have you done now? You have really messed up your life and the lives of your family." This has to be your all-time biggest screw-up," I had wanted "more" but it was looking like "less" as I drifted off to an uneasy sleep.

2

The darkness was giving way to the morning sun. People were starting to wake up and move about the cabin. The overhead lights had been turned on. The kids were still sleeping. I had lost track of time. My watch was still set for New York time, but how many time zones had we passed since then?

The intercom gave the wake-up call. "We will be landing in Dakar, Senegal in about an hour. You will be served breakfast prior to the landing." The kids were waking up. I could see heads moving and arms and legs stretching as if to strain against the noises and sunlight-disturbing sleep. Paula sat up and looked at me with puffy eyes, "Are we in Africa yet?" Beth lifted her head from the pillow and squinted at the light turning back under the blanket with a groan. "I don't want to get up yet." Stephen was looking out the window. "It is all water now." John was still sleeping. Paula pushed her hand against Beth's side, "Beth, look you can see the ocean." Beth reluctantly stretched up and turned her head to look out the window.

The stewardess was pushing a cart down the aisle, reaching into a silver pan with metal tongs, and lifting out a steaming washcloth for each passenger. That looked good. I felt rumpled and dirty. My tongue must have been in the bottom of a bird cage all night. We were all given a hot washcloth. It felt good to wipe my face with this warm cloth. The cloths had a faint order of mint. John started to wake up. He was fighting consciousness. Beth held a cloth under John's nose. "John, smell the washcloth. It smells like gum." The kids started smelling each other's washcloth. After the washcloth smelling, the children all had to go to the bathroom. Joyce took the girls and John. John still wet in his diapers—mother's job.

The area around our seats was cluttered with papers, peanut bags, playing cards, sections of the *New York Times,* children's books, toy cars, dolls, airline blankets, and pillows.

After the children returned from the bathroom, papers, toys, books, blankets, and pillows were put away. The stewardess came down the aisle again with breakfast, and our thoughts and conversation turned to our new life in Africa. The intercom—"We are about to land in Dakar. We should be on the ground in about 15 minutes. Please return to your seats and fasten your seat belts. Make sure your seats are in the upright position. The ground temperature is 78 degrees without a cloud in the sky. Thank you for flying with us."

I could feel the plane's engines backing off to break the speed, and we were coming down. We could see the land now. Sand and palm trees. We had never seen palm trees before. This was exciting. "Look, land. Look, there's the airport."

Landings and takeoffs are the only times the feeling of flight is apparent. The engines roar and the plane shakes. This is followed by the bump, bump, bump of the wheels coming down on the ground. The plane seems to be going too fast on the ground to stop on the runway. There is a deafening roar of the engines as the plane slows down. The plane crawled along the cement path to the terminal. People were starting to stand up and pull luggage down from the compartments overhead. The intercom—"Ladies and Gentlemen we are in Dakar, Senegal. Please remain seated until the plane comes to a full stop." The passengers ignored this request and keep on pulling luggage down. The stewardess stood at the front of the cabin and told everyone to get back in their seats.

The intercom—"We will be in Dakar for about a half hour. You may leave the airplane, but keep your boarding passes." I wanted to get out and see the terminal. It isn't much of a terminal. One single-story building surrounded with sand and the occasional palm tree. I didn't want to take the children with me. It would be too hard to get the kids on and off the plane in a half-hour's time. Mother didn't want to get out of the plane here. So, I left the plane and walked across the runway to the airport.

The terminal is just a cement building with a section for the loading trucks to place luggage. One table serves as a ticket area. There were a few passengers standing around. There was only one white person. The rest were Africans. Each door was guarded by a policeman with a rifle. The rifles had bayonets in place. The policemen were dressed in "army-looking" uniforms. No one spoke English.

There wasn't much to see or do in the terminal. I didn't even see a men's room. It was just a storage area with one door to the runway and another door that opens to nothing. No parking lot, no signs of modern roads—stop signs, traffic lights. Just the desert.

The airplane looked like it was about to take off. I was the only passenger who had gone into the terminal. The rest of the people who got out kept near the airplane. I could see these passengers going back up the steps to the airplane door. It was time to return to the plane. As I approached the door of the terminal, the guard, policeman, or soldier (I was not sure which category this person was in) barred my access to the door and pointed the rifle bayonet at me saying, "Port!" Port? What is port? "That's my airplane. I'm going back to the airplane now," I said. The guard pushed the rifle at me and demanded "PORT!" "I want to go back to my plane," I explained. Now, I was getting nervous. What is "port?" The guard didn't speak English and would not let me pass through the door. Man! I am going to miss the plane. Everyone had gone back into the plane. The doors were still open, but I was the only one out. "I came in on that airplane, and I have to go back now," I explained. "Port!" The guard said. What does this guy want? Port?

The only other white person in the terminal walked over and asked me what the problem was. He sounded like an American. I could have hugged this guy I was so glad he was there. "This guard won't let me return to my airplane, and it's ready to leave." The man spoke to the guard in the guard's language. Wow! What luck. This American must be with the embassy or something. The American turned to me and said, "He wants to see your passport." "Passport?" That must be what he meant by "Port." "My passport? My passport is back in the plane," I explained. I started feeling scared again. The American and the guard talked back and forth again. The American was not doing well, and the airplane was going to be leaving any minute. I was not going to be allowed back on the plane. The American and the guard kept talking and gesturing with their hands. "What's he saying?" I asked. "He says you're not allowed beyond this point without your passport." I could feel a tightening of my throat, and my stomach felt funny. "Look," I said to the American, "I have a wife and four children on that plane. I've got to get back there." The American reached into his pocket and took out his billfold. He showed his billfold to the guard. The guard took a long, slow look at it. "My plane's leaving. I've got to get out there." I said to both of them. The American and the guard continued talking. The stewardess was standing in the door of the plane. They're going to go. I'm missing the plane. The American turned to me and said, "He's going to let you leave. Just get on the plane and don't get off anywhere without your passport and boarding pass." "Thank you," I said, "I mean thank you very much. I mean it." I felt such relief. "O.K. Now just get to your plane." He told me. Running to the airplane I yelled at the stewardess, "Hey! Wait for me. Don't close the door. Wait!" I boarded the plane and got in my seat. Joyce looked at me and said, "Where were you? I thought you were going to miss the plane." "So did I," I replied. "I'm not leaving this plane again until we get to Uganda."

Uganda. I didn't realize that the distance between Dakar, Senegal, and Uganda was farther than the distance between Maine and California. The flight between Senegal and Uganda was a long day, especially traveling with four children. We had a two-hour flight to Monrovia, Liberia; another two-hour flight from Liberia to Accra, Ghana; an hour's flight to Lagos, Nigeria; and then a five-hour flight to Entebbe, Uganda.

There was nothing to do on the plane but listen to music with earphones, play cards with the kids, and read the newspaper—any newspaper. The kids colored, did dot-to-dot in books, ran cars across the seats while kneeling on the floor, ate airplane meals, and argued. "When are we going to get to Uganda?" was the most often asked question. Stephen didn't want to go to Africa. Paula and Beth hated airplanes, and John had grown bored with the bathroom. We stayed on the airplane at the Monrovia, Accra, and Lagos stops. The landscape had changed from that of Dakar, Senegal. The former had been desert—sand with palm trees. The air had felt clean and refreshing. Now the stops were jungle looking with hot, muggy air. The terminals were small and looked like American big city bus stations. They looked dirty and were surrounded by galvanized tin huts, junk cars, and buses.

By the time we had reached Entebbe, Uganda, we all felt wretched. It was late afternoon. of which day? I couldn't remember. What day is it? How long have we been traveling? Well, lets see. We left home yesterday about 10 a.m. and drove three hours to the airport. We got on the plane and flew to Newark Airport. Oh, New York. How I wish I were back in New York. Then we flew from New York to Dakar. The morning felt so good in Dakar. Then jungle, hot, travel. Why did I ever leave home and go to Africa? What a mess! I don't want to be here. I wish I were home. The kids want to go home. My wife, Joyce, never wanted to leave home. Uganda. This is where we get out of the plane.

From the airplane windows, it looked better than Ghana and Nigeria, but not much better. Another roar of engines, another bump, bump, bump. Another intercom—"Thank you for flying with us." The stewardesses looked tired. It was getting evening. We collected the luggage from overhead, the cars, books, and clothes from the seat pockets. We got the kids in line, collected the luggage, tickets, and the passports. African airports are all guarded by soldiers. Are these policemen or soldiers? They all have rifles. Strange.

Customs, Arriving Passengers. We filed through this door and had our passports taken from us. A soldier asked, "What is the purpose of your visit?" He spoke English. Good. "I am, er, we are here to teach at Tororo Girls

School for the University of Massachusetts." I replied. The soldier held his hand out saying. "Give me your work permit." Work permit? What is that? I don't know what he's talking about. That same funny feeling started in my stomach that I had in Dakar over "Port." "I don't have a work permit." I said. "You must have a work permit." the soldier insisted. "Do you work for the American Embassy?" "No," I said, "I'm working for USAID at Tororo Girls School." The soldier called an African man in a blue suit over. They spoke in a combination of English and some other language. The soldier didn't speak English well and had to revert to an African language to explain details. The gentleman in the suit spoke English very well. He had a British accent. He sounded like he was from England. His manner was very kind to us. However, he didn't seem to be familiar with USAID, University of Massachusetts, or any of the other details of my purpose for being in Uganda. The children were getting restless. "Dad, I have to go to the bathroom." It was John again.

The African in the suit, the soldier, and I were reaching the point of complete misunderstanding. How do I get out of here and to Tororo Girls School? From across the room I saw an American woman talking with another blue-suited African. They were walking toward us with a purpose. Maybe this is the woman from Tororo Girls School who is supposed to meet us. Maybe this is—What is the name of the woman who is going to meet us? Oh, yes, Mary, Mary Riley.

3

Mary Riley breezed in, took control of the situation, and led us through airport customs like Moses led the children of Israel through the Red Sea. The custom officials said, "This man needs a work permit." Mary Riley took care of that, and we passed through without the need of a work permit. The custom officials said, "All luggage brought into this country must be inspected." Mary Riley took care of that, and we passed though without any inspection. Mary Riley gave orders and directed the entire process of our passage through the airport. She just told the officials what to do, and they did it.

There is only one hotel at Entebbe. We could have driven to the capital city of Kampala, but Entebbe is the city by the airport. Mary drove us to the hotel and got us into our room She had made reservations for us. The hotel was laid out in the shape of a C with a swimming pool and patio in the middle. Our room had green and yellow painted cement walls and high ceilings with a big fan in the center. It looked like a hospital room with six double-size beds. There were no pictures on the cement walls. The top half was painted light yellow, and the bottom half of the wall was painted light green. The floors were also cement. This cement was polished with wax and covered by a braided cloth rug.

It was only about 8 p.m., but we were exhausted and too sick to feel hungry, so we went to our room and went to bed. The last thing I had to do before turning out the light was kill a huge cockroach that was crawling across the floor. "Look at the size of that cockroach," Joyce screamed. Yuk! It was as big as a half dollar. I stepped on it and cleaned the floor with a tissue. I went to sleep wishing I had never agreed to come to this place. Two years. What a mess!

The next morning I discovered that our room didn't have a bath connected. In Uganda, from its British influence, one does not have a "bathroom" one has a "toilet." Anyway, we didn't have one. If you had to use the toilet, it was at the end of the hall. Four sleeping rooms, one toilet.

The hotels in Uganda have breakfast included in the price of the room. Orange or tomato juice. Scrambled or fried eggs. Toast, smaller sliced, thicker, and standing in little racks to make sure it is cold, and bacon. English-style bacon is not really well done and the fat is not fried away. The children had cereal—Rice Krispies or corn flakes. The food is served by waiters dressed in white, starched cotton uniforms.

After breakfast we went outside to the patio area. This was the center of the C-shape building layout. There were patio waiters in uniforms just like those in the dining room. Some of the guests were having tea by the pool. We were just waiting by the pool wondering when Mary Riley would appear. There was a big turtle foraging around the flower beds and lawn. It was the biggest turtle I had ever seen. Well, that was something. The biggest cockroach and the biggest turtle all in less than 24 hours.

The kids were in much better shape than my wife or I were. They were having a grand time running around the flower beds, petting the turtle, and watching the monkeys in the trees. I was hardly able to sit in the chair. I didn't even want tea. I just wanted to go home. Joyce looked like I felt—sick.

"Hey, Dad, can we go in the pool?" Stephen said. "Yea, yea, the pool," the girls said. John didn't like pools. He was afraid of water. I didn't know how one got permission to use the pool, and I wanted to be ready to go when Mary Riley appeared. "I don't think we should go in the pool now," I said. "We have to be ready to go when Miss Riley comes." I should have let them use the pool, but it cost a shilling for each person, and I didn't have any shillings or know how much that was. It was all too confusing for me, and I couldn't deal with the pool. It was too early to "pool" anyway.

About ten thirty Mary Riley showed up. We got our luggage packed in the car and started the four-hour drive to Tororo Girls School. The drive took us through Kampala, the capital city, and then east. It was not jungle, and we did not see any elephants, lions, or giraffe. There were a lot of people walking along the road. The men were riding bicycles, while the women and children walked. Most of the men wore khaki shorts and short-sleeved shirts. The women wore long, ankle-length dresses. Several of the women had rust-colored clay pots on their heads. Some had pots on their heads as well as a baby strapped to their back.

We crossed Owen Falls Dam at Jinja. Owen Falls Dam is located on the north end of Lake Victoria. Lake Victoria rushes through Owen Falls Dam into the Nile River on its way through Egypt to the Mediterranean Ocean. Jinja is a small town located on the banks of Lake Victoria next to Owen Falls Dam. The spray of the water from Owen Falls Dam causes a continual rainbow.

We stopped at a tea room next to the dam on Lake Victoria. The Tea Room had a patio which looked out on lake shore. It was hard to find something on the menu that the kids would like to eat. There were no hamburgs or french fries—definitely not a McDonald's. There were no hot dogs. In fact, it would be two years before we ever saw a hot dog again. In retrospect, I am not able to say if that was a curse or a blessing. The most popular menu item was fish and chips. Potato chips are called "krisps" and french fries are called "chips." However, British-style french fries (excuse me, chips) are much thicker than American french fries. Another American favorite, peanut butter, is also absent from Ugandan restaurant menus and grocery stores. About the only menu items that the children were familiar with were spaghetti or cheese sandwiches.

After lunch at Jinja we had another hour or so drive to Tororo Girls School and our new home. The traffic on the road was as interesting as the people walking along it. There were a lot of lorries. "Lorry" is a British name for a truck. Most of these lorries seemed to be sagging on one side and were belching black, foul-smelling smoke. There were also many busses. The busses sagged also. Most of these were painted yellow and red. Each bus had a roof rack which was piled high with bicycles, boxes tied with hemp rope, wicker baskets with chickens, and huge bunches of bananas. The bananas grown in Uganda are about half the size of those sold in the States, but are much sweeter. The most common banana found in Uganda is a cooking banana, which the Africans call "matoke" (MAA-TOE-KEY). These are cooked and eaten while the peel is green. If matoke is eaten without cooking one becomes quite sick with stomach cramps.

As we traveled to Tororo, which is the town from which Tororo Girls School got its name, we could see acres and acres of sugar cane. The sugar cane fields are divided into sections by irrigation ditches. These irrigation ditches are full of red-colored water. The water is red from the soil, which is a bright rust color. After we had passed the sugar cane plantations, we drove through miles and miles of banana trees and African huts. These huts were one of two styles. The traditional African dwelling is round with a thatch roof. The round bottom section is made by mixing the rust-colored soil and cow manure with water and then plastering tree limbs with this mixture. When it dries, it becomes a thick wall that supports the thatch roof. The modern style of building is square. These square walls are made of tree limbs, again plastered with this mud-cow manure mixture. However, the square houses have a galvanized tin roof which looks much the same as American-style roofs. These buildings are all single-story dwellings. These African homes do not have grass around them. The dirt about the homes is beaten flat and does not have any grass or bushes. It is like cement. This keeps snakes and bugs away from the dwelling. There are always children, of all ages, on the roads and around these huts. The only children that attend school are those whose parents can afford the required school fees. So, most African children do not attend school.

The African huts we passed did not have electricity, running water, or even glass in the windows. The cooking and bathing were done outside of the dwelling.

These scenes would have been interesting to watch on a film, but this was not a film for us. This was our life. This was the neighborhood—where we lived. Africa! The elephants, the lions, the giraffe. We still had not seen these. Africa! The foul-smelling lorries, the decrepit-looking buses, the homes without electricity, or bathrooms (excuse me, toilets), the red muddy irrigation ditches, the cockroaches, the filth, the smells. Africa, my home. I felt depressed. Two years of this. What had I gotten my family into? How stupid to come here. I was sick over the conditions I saw around us. Joyce looked sick also. The kids seemed fine. "Hey, Beth, Paula, look at the size of the pot on that woman's head." Stephen was saying. "Look at the chickens that woman has in the basket on her head, Stephen," Beth said. "Goats," John said, "Goats."

4

"There's Tororo Girls School," Mary Riley said. We had just crossed the top of a small hill, and a view of the African plain for ten miles opened to us. On the right side of the road were the school and faculty houses. It seemed so out of place after the miles of banana trees and native huts. We were looking down at something that resembled a small American college. There were eight large, two-story block buildings. They were grey cement structures in a square surrounding an open grass area. In the middle of the grass area there was a tall water tower with a big clock at the top. The sidewalk around the edge of the center grass area was covered with a roof. At one end there was a big outdoor gym also covered by a roof. At the other end were seven ranch-style houses. It looked as though someone had taken a piece of Southern California and placed it in the middle of Africa.

Our house was the fourth one. These houses were exact duplicates of each other. The houses were divided into two sections with a connecting breezeway. One section contained a kitchen, dining room, and living room. The living room had a sliding glass door which opened onto a patio. The bedrooms and bathroom were across the breezeway in the other section. These houses had large grass lawns with fruit trees and a five-foot tall hedge along the side next to the road. The houses were constructed of cement. The outside walls were painted yellow over a stucco-type surface.

Our sea freight had not arrived yet with the two thousand pounds of personal goods we had packed back in New York. The house was, however, completely furnished. So, we were able to unpack our luggage and feel right at home.

The children were roaming through the house, trying the beds, turning on the water, flushing the toilet, opening the refrigerator and oven. "Which is my bedroom, Dad?" Stephen asked. We decided on bedrooms for the two boys and two girls. There were three bedrooms. One for mom and dad, one for the girls, and one for the boys.

A car pulled in the driveway, and out stepped an American. "Hi. I am George Andrezejewski. This is my wife, Joan, and our children Alexander and Alyessia. We live in the last house down. If there's anything you need, just give a yell and we'll help. I see you have, how many—two, three, four—children? My God! don't know why U. Mass would send a family with four children here. You kids be careful outside on the lawn. There are snakes all over. You've got to be careful of the snakes. There are cobras, and the three-steppers." George looked at me with raised eyebrows and said, "You'll learn about three-steppers. If one of those babies bite you, you get three steps before you're gone; and USAID ships you home in body bag. The water! Don't drink the water. That's a more painful death than the snake bite. I hate to even bathe in the water. Sometimes it gets as dark as coffee. Oh, yea, and be sure to lock your doors at night. We've got thieves here that will take the shirt off your back when you're sleeping. God! I don't know why a man with four children would ever come to a place like this. Didn't Doubleday warn you? I had a car accident the first day I got my car. You can see they drive on the opposite side of the road from the States—like England. We were just about killed our first day here.

"If I could have turned around and gone back home then, I would have. You've got to be careful driving. People here aren't used to cars. They'll run across the road in front of you. Man, I'll tell you, it's terrible. If you ever hit someone, don't stop. Just keep driving to the next town, and tell the police. If you stop, you'll be stoned to death."

This nonstop dialogue on the dangers of African living was making me feel depressed. I hadn't thought about snakes, water, car accidents, and thieves. Oh, Man! What had I gotten into? Mary Riley said, "George, give it a rest. If this is such a bad place, why have you been here longer than anyone else on staff? I've never heard of anyone being bitten by a snake. No one's home has been broken into, and I don't know of anyone who has gotten sick from the water. Everyone knows you boil and filter."

As George was delivering his "Beware of Uganda" presentation; a man, woman, and three young boys had entered the house. "Hi! I'm Bill Gatchell. This is my wife, Ellen, and our three boys, Carl, Philip, and Douglas. Don't listen to George here. He 'loves' Uganda—Don't you, George."

However, George was right about automobile accidents. Soon after we arrived in Tororo, the *Uganda Argus* carried the following story about an accident in which an African girl was hit by a car:

OCCUPANTS STONED AS CAR KILLS GIRL

Stones were hurled at a car that knocked down and killed a seven-year-old girl on the Turbo-Eldoret road on

Saturday. The driver and his two passengers had to be treated for injuries.

Mr. S. Hoelgaard and his wife, who went to the rescue of the driver, were admitted to Mount Elgon hospital after they were seriously injured by the stone throwers.

The "Rules of the Road" were different in Uganda. If you hit someone, DON'T STOP!!! If you stop, people will stone you to death.

The Gatchell children were about the same ages as ours. The Gatchell boys were showing our children around the house and yard. "Hey kids," I shouted, "be careful of snakes. Don't go near the hedges." Bill Gatchell put his hand on my shoulder, "They'll be alright, my boys are outside all the time. They explore around the school, down the road. They'll be O.K."

We were pretty well settled in with the exception of our sea freight and car. I was told that it would about six weeks before these arrived.

One of the first things we had to do was to get groceries. Gatchell drove us into town. The school was located about a mile or so from "Tororo town," as the two parallel streets of shops are called.

The road running past the TGS houses was only a stone's throw from the main road upon which we had arrived from Kampala. Our "mirrum" road (dirt road) turned off the "tarmac" road (blacktop). (More new British words.) Our murrum road continued past the Tororo Girls School faculty houses and into the banana trees and African huts until it ended at a river about a half mile off. This river was about 100 feet wide with a 10- to 15-foot deep rushing current of rust-colored water. Crocodiles were seen from time to time sunning themselves on the banks with their mouths open. These crocks looked like big transport ships with loading doors propped open awaiting cargo.

Gatchel drove us up to the main road, which never seemed to be busy with automobile traffic. There were always African men and bicycles. "Men and bicycles, not "Men on bicycles." Africans use bicycles, for the most part, to carry loads—bananas, chickens, etc. I never saw women on or with bicycles. Bicycles were for men not women or children.

As we turned left onto the main road, I noticed a hotel. "The Rock" hotel was one of a chain of 13 hotels scattered across the countryside of Uganda. These hotels are stopping places for travelers which are located between distant points and in Game Parks. This "Rock" hotel was in Tororo which is midpoint between Kenya's capital of Nairobi and the Uganda capital of Kampala. It contained a dining room/bar combination, banquet rooms, pool, and rooms for about 50 guests. The Rock's buildings were white stucco with bougainvillea-covered walls, nicely trimmed lawns landscaped with miniature banana groves, and little islands of flowers. The name "Rock Hotel" was because of the large extinct volcano core nearby, which looked much like those in the Four-Corners area of New Mexico.

The road into "Tororo Town" provided the only "tarmac" corners for more than an hour's drive in either direction. On this corner was the only gas, "petrol," station in the same distance.

Gatchell took a right at the corner, and drove up a hill. At the top of this hill Tororo Girls School was visible a mile to the south, and The Rock and Tororo Town could be seen a mile to the north. The road leading into town was lined by tall, broad trees with purple flowers. The air was crisp and dry, the sun was shining, and there were flowers of every description on either side of road.

The road to town became a "street" to town as we traveled down the hill. There were houses with cars parked in driveways, tarmac streets, utility poles, street lights, and other signs of "European" influence. "European." All white people in Uganda are European to the Africans. It was impossible to explain that Americans do not come from Europe. We all look the same. If you've seen one European, you've seen them all.

As we neared the town center, the street became more urban/commercial. We passed a post office on the left, and soccer field on the right. We also drove by the police station, which does not have a police-car parking lot. The Ugandan Police ride bicycles. There were more people along the street nearer the center of town. Town people dress in brighter colors than village people. In villages we had seen men in white shirts with khaki shorts, and women wearing long, drab-colored dresses. Here in town the dress was of greater variety, and more colorful. There are also "European" people both walking and driving cars. This drive town made me feel more "at home" than the drive from the airport.

The main street of Tororo had two grocery stores, a garage for auto repair, a travel agency, and a hardware store that bore a sign which read: *G. K. Patel, Iron Monger*. The businesses were predominantly owned by Asians. "Asian" is the name given to people whose ancestors came from India. When Kenya and Uganda were English colonies, the British brought people from India to build the East African Railway system. These Indians stayed in East Africa and became the merchants. These Asians, even though born in East Africa, held British passports.

The Asians had done very well in East Africa. They were the owners of most businesses and the professional people—lawyers, teachers, and doctors. They knew, however, that their days were numbered. When Uganda and Kenya became independent from England, black Africans wanted to rid themselves of the Asians and take over their businesses. Most Asians had British bank accounts and were sending money out of the country.

The Gatchells took us to Tororo General Store and introduced us to Mr. Patel, the Asian owner. Tororo General was a small store with only one room about 20-foot square. The groceries were on shelves that went from floor to ceiling on both sides of the room.

Tororo General did not carry eggs, milk, or meat. There is a government-owned Uganda Milk Supply. Since this milk is unpasteurized, it is not considered safe to drink by most Europeans. Meat came from a local outdoor market. The meat is displayed on tables in the open-air market and covered with flies.

When purchased, it is wrapped in newspaper by the vendor. The printer's ink transfers from this newspaper to the meat. Bill Gatchell said: "You can read the newspaper and eat dinner at the same time without others noticing."

Once a week, usually on a Saturday, TGS faculty took turns driving to Nairobi, Kenya, and brought back milk and meat for the American faculty and staff at TGS. The milk in Kenya is pasteurized in such a way as to not require refrigeration. Kenya meat is the same quality as that purchased in the States.

One problem with groceries is their age. Most of the packaged food comes from England or Australia. Tomatoes and fruit juices in cans "tins" are a problem. When purchasing tinned items, one pushes on the end of the container with the thumbs. If the tin pushes back with a "POP," it is spoiled. Pushing a can opener into one of these "poppers" would result in an explosion that would cover the ceiling, walls, counters, and even the person with the contents of the can.

With the help of the Gatchells, we brought a small quantity of "staples" needed to start housekeeping.

As we were leaving Tororo General Store, Mr. Patel put his arm around my shoulder and said, "I am very happy to be meeting you today and am thanking you for your businesses with Tororo General Store. I am looking forward to bringing you many fine items for your consumption while you are staying in Tororo. And, Mr. Gatchell, I am thanking you also for bringing your friend into our store. We are all being at your service, please."

5

The first two weeks at Tororo Girls School were an entire reorganization of our lives. We wanted to set up a personal schedule prior to the start of classes. The students were due back on September 1. We had arrived in country the first week in August. That gave us just four weeks to get our new lives in order.

By the end of the first week in Uganda we had moved into our furnished home, met those American staff not on school vacation, and stocked our home with food staples and household items we had expected, as well as those we had not expected. What a list! It seemed that every day we were making notes of new things we had never dreamed of needing.

For example, the American electrical appliances we had brought could not be used. The British system of electricity is 240 volts, not the 110 volts our appliances were made for. Hair dryers, electric razors, radios, tape players, toasters, mixers—the list went on and on—were useless. We had known about this electrical difference, but had been told that we would be able to purchase "adapters" that would convert the 240 house current to the 110 needed. That is true. However, we would need at least three of these adapters in every room. The small, convenient-size adapters did not work well and soon burned out. The more reliable models are the size of a small loaf of bread, are quite heavy, and very expensive in Uganda.

TGS staff were originally supplied with one of these better adapters per house. However, during the first three or four years of the Uganda Project, many of these converters had been stolen, lost, or broken. When staff returned to the States, they would bequeath these valuable converters to their colleagues who were remaining at TGS. So, in actuality, very few converters were available. The best thing to do was buy British-style appliances from others who were at the end of their tour and leaving country.

There was about a 30 to 50 percent staff turnover each year. Most staff left at the end of their original two-year hitch. Families signed on for a two-year assignment. The first year they were adjusting to living in Africa. The second year they were helping the new people adjust to their first year of African living. Then they went back to the States. It was funny, really—the first year learning to deal with such a different way of life, being homesick, and needing the help of the "old timers" (the ones with a year's experience) and the second year laughing at new people who came the year after when you were an "old timer." There were those who stayed on and on—like George Andrezejewski. George never had many positive things to say about TGS, Africa, Uganda, USAID, or U. Mass., but he kept coming back for more. Like a man who is always complaining about his wife, but never gets a divorce. George fought with Africa, and complained about how bad it was to live in Africa, but could never quite leave her.

The lawns around the houses were well kept. George had warned me about snakes. Bill Gatchell had said there was not a snake problem—just keep your grass cut short. This was hard to do without a lawn mower. None of the houses had lawn mowers. The lawn mowing was accomplished by the "lawn man." We were the "new family" in house four and would be needing two employees: One person to work outside—lawn mowing, car washing, gardening, tree and shrub care, and snake killing; and one person (man or woman) for inside work—cleaning, laundry, kitchen duties, and child care.

This was a new concept to my wife and me. We had never had what the British called "servants" in the States. Once in a while, I had paid a boy to mow the lawn, or a girl to babysit children while we were away from home. Why would we need two full-time employees here in Uganda? However, we really did have several full-time employees in the States. Their names were Hoover, Craftsman, Whirlpool, Maytag, and one who was referred to by his initials—GE.

It just was not practical to have appliances in Tororo. We were only going to be there two years. The initial expense of purchase was too great. Only "rich" people had appliances in Africa. The "poor" folk had servants. Then, too, who would repair broken machines? Where could one buy parts for these repairs? Major appliances in Africa were just not practical or available to us.

On our first full day at TGS, a large crowd of men were lined up outside our front door looking for work. I felt like the personnel manager of some large corporation. Most of these job hunters came equipped with letters from former employers, but were unable to speak more than a few words of English. With the help of the "old timers" we were able to choose two men—Francis for inside work, and Onyango for outside work. After that, when people came looking for work, I would just send Francis out to explain that we didn't need any more help.

House and lawn work kept Francis and Onyango busy all day long. For example, the cement floors of the entire house were polished every week. We had to buy polishing slippers for Francis. These were all wool and three times the size of average slippers. Francis removed everything out of a room; put wax, like car polish, on the floor, put on these slippers, and would scuff about the room until the floor was clean and bright.

Mowing the lawn was just as difficult. Since lawn mowers were not available, the grass cutting had to be done with something that resembled a golf club. Arnold Palmer would have excelled at this work. Onyango walked about the lawn swinging this "golf club" slasher with vigor. Then he raked the lawn of the grass clippings and put them in a pile for garden mulch. This outside job had a bonus. For every snake the garden man killed and brought to me, he was paid 15 bob. "Bob" was the English term for shilling. This 15 bob represented 10 percent of his week's salary, or about $2.50.

The English complained that the Americans were paying their servants too much and spoiling the job market. I paid Francis and Onyango both $25 each week for six, eight-hour days.

Appliance purchase in the States, plus energy, plus repair would have cost about the same as I paid the servants to do this work. My savings was entirely that of time.

American staff were expected to have servants at TGS. Each house had a separate servant's quarters building. We were bringing money to the local economy, and Americans were paying more than other Europeans. We paid so little, but still were paying much higher than these men could have earned anywhere else in Uganda.

The house was furnished, the food supply was stocked, the work of maintaining the house was taken care of, we had nice neighbors, and I had a job. What was left? The children! What do children do? They go to school! Children go to the local grammar, secondary, or high school provided by the government. WRONG! Children in Africa stay home or go to the school that mom and dad can pay for. The Ugandan government didn't provide education.

There was no American School in Tororo. However, there was a school taught by Asians. Remember "Asians?" Well, the only education available to our children was a school that the Asian community provided for Asian children and anyone else who could pay the school fees. Since my contract provided for child education expenses, we enrolled Stephen, grade three; Paula, grade two; and Beth, grade one in the local Asian school. John stayed home with mom.

6

There was not a lot to do in Tororo. Television and local radio were not available. Most staff had a shortwave radio and listened to the BBC (British Broadcasting Corporation), the American Armed Forces Network, or the Voice of America. I thought the BBC was best. That station had a little more variety. The Voice of America was the worst. "This is the Voice of America, coming to you in Special English."

Special English was for persons with a limited English vocabulary and was spoken V-E-R-Y S-L-O-W-L-Y.

I could appreciate the "very slowly." We were trying to learn a bit of Swahili. I wrote down Swahili words phonetically and then practiced saying them to myself. When I listened to Swahili being spoken, I recognized the words, but they seemed to be coming so fast that I would become lost. I should have had a program coming to me in S-P-E-C-I-A-L S-W-A-H-I-L-I. Children seemed to pick up the language quicker than adults. I have heard British and American adults ask their children to give instructions to the servants. I once found Francis in the kitchen preparing scrambled eggs. John, age 4, had told Francis, "Mimi nataka mieye." (I want eggs.) I don't think John was actually hungry, he just liked being able to tell Francis to do something in Swahili. I told Francis, "The next time John asks you to fix scrambled eggs, ask my wife or me first."

As the Africans went about their household chores, the small children walked around the house with them talking. The Africans were good with children, and the kids seemed to enjoy their company. There was a word game that these house servants played with the children. It was a "Where is?" followed by a "Here is." dialogue. The houseboy or housegirl would say "Wapi" (where is) "ma junga" (the orange). The child would point and reply. "Hapa" (here is) "ma junga" (the orange). It would go on and on: "Wapi kitabu?" "Where is the book?" The child would point and say "Hapa kitabu." "Here is the book." Through the day the child would follow the teacher accumulating a great store of nouns that were soon put together in sentences.

Tororo had a "mixed bag" of nations represented. There were British, German, Dutch, French, Australian, Indian, and Americans living in and around the town.

These "Europeans" had a country club. Without television, theater, or any other form of entertainment, "The Club" was about the only place to go. It had a golf course, tennis courts, swimming pool, and a club house.

We didn't play golf or tennis; but, spent a lot of time at the pool. The kids were just learning to swim, so, The Club was a family swimming pool for us. It was a small pool, but provided an activity for the entire family.

There was one very important thing to remember when swimming in the pool. Don't leave anything outside the car. Any clothing, eye glasses, toys, lunch baskets, etc. were quickly stolen by baboons. These baboons would swing down from the trees, grab anything left unguarded, and bound off through the jungle with it. Beth lost a pair of sunglasses to a baboon that way. She put her sunglasses down and jumped into the pool. Before I could yell

"Beth, remember to keep your glasses," a baboon was running off through the jungle with them.

In addition to The Club, there was a chess night. Some Dutch and German priests drove 20 miles to attend chess night. Every Wednesday evening some of the Europeans would get together to play chess and listen to classical music. Chess and classical music were international social activities that we all enjoyed. It was a traveling activity and was at the home of a different family each week.

As the days grew into weeks, life in Africa took on a routine. The children had grown used to their new friends and spent a lot of time next door at Gatchell's house. The Gatchell children had been in Uganda for more than a year. During this time they had accumulated a lot of "neat things." They had also learned a lot of "neat things." One of their favorite games was "centipede hockey." The cement floors of the houses were polished with wax each week. This made them smooth and slippery, which provided an excellent playing field for centipede hockey games. There were dozens of centipedes in the flower beds just outside the houses. These hard-shelled centipedes were about two inches long, and would curl up when touched; forming a tight, little puck about the size of a quarter. The kids would collect these centipedes and snap them along the wax surface of the floor with their finger. The game might be, who can snap the centipede puck the longest distance, or get his centipede puck into the circle, or hit your centipede puck with mine, or any of the several variations possible. The only rule we had at our house was, "Don't forget to take your centipedes with you when you leave!" I hated stepping on centipede pucks!

The students were about to return to school, and we

were ready for the semester to begin. Life had taken on a pattern that was easy to follow. Up every morning at 6:30 a.m., shower, have breakfast, walk out the back door to Tororo Girls School, and into the world of African Academia.

It seemed that every day was bright and sunny. Uganda is on the equator, but has an altitude of over 4,000 feet. That means that the days are never hot and always about 12 hours long—7 a.m. to 7 p.m.—year round. There is a rainy season, when it rains in the afternoon. The temperature is always in the 70s. When Winston Churchill was touring the British Colonies, he called Uganda "The Pearl of Africa."

There were two teachers in the Business Department—myself and Isabele Deskins, a single, black American woman from Washington. Isabele seemed to me to be like a black "Aunty Mamie." She had a quick wit and a motherly way with the students. What I remember most about Isabele was the painting she had in her TGS apartment. It was of a naked, black woman resting on a couch with a bird perched on an outstretched hand. The naked woman in the painting looked just like Isabele to me, but I didn't know her well enough to ask if she were the model.

Isabele was an "old timer" who had about the same longevity as George Andrezejewski (ANDREW - F - SKI). She told me that she came to Africa to find her roots and ended up feeling that she was more American than African.

I was scheduled to teach an introduction to business course, a typewriting course, and a shorthand course. When Uganda became independent from Britain, the Africans wanted to fill Ugandan office positions with their own people. "Africa for and by Africans." was a statement that I read more than once in the *Uganda Argus,* the national newspaper.

The Tororo Girls School teaching staff was a "mixed" group. Some of the teachers were white American men with families. In fact, the University of Massachusetts had an unwritten rule that only married men could be hired for the TGS project. I found out later, in talking with Doubleday, that was why I had gotten the job so easily. Elwyn had hired a man for my job before I ever applied. Before this man left for Uganda, Elwyn found out that the man had gotten a divorce and would be a single man on staff. So, the man was denied the job, and a frantic search for a replacement had been started when I applied. It was also the reason that Doubleday drove to my home for the interview rather than interview me in Amherst. He wanted to be sure that I was married. USAID did not want a single man living with a school full of African women. I am sure that was a wise choice.

In addition to married men, white and black, there were single American women, white and black, and Ugandan men and women. Some of the African faculty were married and some were single women. Again, no single African men. I am sure that was wise also.

The principal of the school was a white, single woman, Phyllis Roop. Her title was officially, "Headmistress. " She had a great deal of fun with that. She also said that her name spelled backward was "Poor."

Most of the American staff were USAID people, but there were also some Peace Corps personnel—a couple of young women and a retired man and his wife from Oklahoma. They were both retired teachers. When they retired from teaching in Oklahoma, they joined the Peace Corps.

The Business Manager, Don Williams, was an American from Arizona. He was married with three young boys, about 3, 7, and 9 years old.

The faculty was becoming more and more Ugandan. Each year TGS sent its best students to the University of Massachusetts to work on a degree in education and return to teach at TGS. The plan was to eventually staff the school entirely with Ugandans. When I arrived, the faculty was about half American, half African.

7

Girls started arriving early in the morning and continued throughout the day. The school was designed for over 400 students. These girls came from all parts Uganda. Although the country was small—approximately the size of Britain—there were sixteen major tribes and several other smaller tribes. Each of these tribes had a distinct language and customs.

When placing girls in dormitories, it was important to consider what tribe these girls came from. If there were two girls of the same tribe in a dorm room of four students, these girls would speak to each other in their tribal language. This caused a problem with the other girls who did not understand the language. Students came to me with the complaint, "Those two are backbiting me. Make them speak English."

Although it was not practical or possible to keep girls of the same tribe from speaking together in tribal language, we did our best to eliminate the opportunity by separating girls from the same tribe as much as possible.

Tribe was very important to the students. These girls did not think of themselves as "Ugandans," they thought of themselves as "Buganda," "Basoga," "Lango," or any one of the other twenty-some tribes. When introducing themselves, they would always say, for example: "My name is Euleni Nabwire, and I am Basama by tribe." It was always that way, "My name is . . . and my tribe is."

The president of the country, Milton Obote, who is Lango by tribe, overthrew Uganda's King Freddie, who was Buganda by tribe. This meant that it would not be good to put a Lango girl in the same dormitory room with a Buganda girl. The tribal war that Milton Obote's Lango tribe had with King Freddie's Buganda tribe was a good subject to stay away from. The Buganda whispered "Kabaka Yakal" to each other. It meant "The King Only."

It is not "Mr." Milton Obote, it is "Dr." Milton Obote. I asked my class, "What does President Obote have a doctorate in?" The Buganda girls yelled back at me, "He is a Doctor of Murder and Stealing!" When King Freddie escaped to England and Obote assumed the position of president, one of his first acts was to imprison all Buganda people with an education. All Buganda lawyers, doctors, teachers, and members of parliament. These people were not charged with a crime, but they were held in "detention." Educated Buganda were a threat to the Lango President.

In fact, even green and white colors were a threat to Dr. Obote's UPC party. These were the colors of the Democratic Party, which opposed Dr. Obote. Wearing green and white clothing could get one in trouble, as can be seen in this *Uganda Argus* article:

DP SHIRT MAN JAILED

Vicenti Kagombero, who was found wearing a white and green D.P. shirt at a public place in Kayunga, Bugerere, during the emergency, was sent to jail for four months at Kayunga District Court by the Magistrate, Mr. Husein Sengendo.

The man told the magistrate that he did not know that the shirt was in Democratic Party colors, but the magistrate told him that ignorance of the law was no excuse.

There was another article in the *Argus* about green and white colors. Even road signs were not allowed to have these colors.

JINJA "NO" TO GREEN AND WHITE

New road signs in Jinja which have been made in green and white, are being changed to other colors because they have been described as the colors of the Democratic Party.

The Town Clerk of Jinja, Mr. Z. K. Nsaja, said yesterday that the order for the sign boards was made early last year. The colors were those which have been internationally approved as the best ones for the road signs.

"The producers were not aware that the colors would be objectionable in Uganda and when they arrived in Jinja it was not immediately realized by the Department concerned that these were DP colors," he added.

"When this was pointed out at a recent meeting of the Works Committee, a resolution was made to remove them without delay. This is now being done."

He said the action was taken before a recent statement was issued on the matter by Mr. Lyavala-Lwanga, a local UPC leader.

The students had to wear TGS uniforms according to the color of their level. First-year students were blue, second year were yellow, third year were green, and fourth year were rose colored.

The uniform was a cotton knee-length dress with buttons up the entire length of the front and short sleeves.

The girls in my Typewriting I class had blue uniforms and were, therefore, first-year students. There were a lot of things we had to learn about each other. First—one must greet the class with a "Good morning, class." Followed by a "Good Morning, Mr. Stewart."

I had a class list, but I had been warned not to count the students in such a way that they realized they were being counted. Africans say that counting your children is pride and God will take one from you if you count. When asking Ugandan adults the number of children they have, they will probably lie and give you a lower than actual number. They say it is "pride," and that God will punish it.

Where do you start with a student who has never seen a typewriter? Well, I decided to start by demonstrating the use of the typewriter. I called their attention to the teacher's typewriter stand at the front of the room upon which sat a typewriter like the one on their desks. I inserted a sheet of paper and typed a few words on it. Then the paper was removed and passed around the class. One girl said, "I have always wondered how someone could print so nicely for newspapers!"

The rest of that hour was spent on learning how to put a sheet of paper in and remove the paper from the typewriter. In fact, it took two class periods to accomplish this.

The introduction to business class was a lecture class which used a British book. The book used an example of a department store to teach business functions. Page one had a photograph of a department store in England with cars and people passing by, and a flag on the rooftop flag pole. The first chapter was devoted to the organization chart of a department store with the president at the top followed by department managers and sales people.

After we had covered the material I gave a test on the

My typing class.

department store. I asked the question; "What is at the top of the organizational chart of a department store?" The answer that I got most often was, "The flag." Perhaps it was my accent, perhaps it was their poor English skills, perhaps it was their lack of ever having seen or heard of anything like a department store. Most of these girls came from parts of Uganda where the only buildings were mud and thatch huts. Perhaps it was a combination of all of this.

    One dark day during the rainy season, I asked the class, "Would someone please turn on the lights?" No one moved. Everyone just stared at me. So, I repeated in "Special English" "P-L-E-A-S-E T-U-R-N O-N T-H-E L-I-G-H-T-S." Again, no one moved. So, I said in Swahili

"Sako a Taa." (Hit the light.) And a student turned on the light. At that point I wondered just how well the students understood what I was saying. English was not the students' second language, it was, at best, their third. Their first language was their tribal language, the second language was Swahili. Swahili was the trade language. With so many tribal languages in the country, everyone in town spoke Swahili. Arabs brought Swahili to Africa, and it continued as the method by which different tribes communicated with each other. Then English came along as the language of education. The British brought English to the colony and it was the medium of educational exchange in schools.

The third class I had each day was a Gregg shorthand class. This was almost impossible to teach. Imagine using strange symbols to record the sounds of a third language.

By the end of the second week, I had just about given up on ever being able to teach Africans typewriting, shorthand, or business principles. "Bill," I said to Gatchell, "It doesn't seem as though the students are making any progress at all in these classes." "Listen," he replied, "Think of it this way, anything you do is better than nothing. The alternative to TGS is sitting around the village or digging in the garden."

8

"The children are having a party tomorrow in school." My wife was saying. "It's for an Asian holy day, I think. It's called Diwali. Have you ever heard of that?" "Diwali?" I said, "Diwali? What's Diwali?" "I don't know," Joyce said, but they have some kind of a party, and set off firecrackers."

None of the kids had any idea of the meaning of or reason for Diwali and firecrackers, but they were excited about it. I had doubts about the wisdom of sending the kids to Tororo Primary School. The children were being taught English from turbaned teachers who did not speak English in their homes. They were being taught the history of India and Africa, and now Diwali. I was never given a reason for Diwali, it just was a time for setting off fireworks. The dictionary says it is a "Hindu festival of lights, celebrated as a religious holiday throughout India in mid-November."

Mr. Patel at Tororo General Store was excited about Diwali. He was a Sikh. "Oh, Mr. Stewart," he beamed as I went into Tororo General, "You must come with me to see the temple. Come, come, this way." We went out the back door of Tororo General across and down an alley to a white, one-story building. "Now here you must take off your shoes. Leave them right here. No one will take them. We must remove shoes from our feet as we enter the temple."

Inside the door was a room approximately 20 by 20. It was decorated with red and gold curtains. There were two statues, one at either end of the room. The statues were unlike anything I had seen before. One had a man's body sitting with palms up. The head of the body was that of an elephant. The second statue was a man's body in a dancing position. This statue had a monkey's head. Mice were carved at the foot of the statues. At the foot of the statutes were small dishes of oil with a candlewick burning in them. On the floor in front of the statues was all kinds of food.

"These foods are being sacrificed to our gods. Then, we have a festival and eat the foods." The food on the floor in front of the statues seemed to be cakes and cookies, fried rice with chili peppers. The room smelled of curry and baked goods. "Mr. Patel," I asked, "What is Diwali, and what are these statues of?" "I am not sure what the names of the statues are," he explained, "but these came from India many years ago, and each year we celebrate these statues with a festival and fireworks." None of the Asians in Tororo seemed to know the reason for Diwali, or the reason for the statues, or the meanings of Sikh celebrations. My best guess is that when these people left India, they brought their Sikh religion and traditions with them. Through the years the meanings of these things had been lost, and all that remained was the festival and the firecrackers. No one seemed to care about the reasons, they were just enjoying the festival and the fireworks. I received a "Happy Diwali" card from an Asian student at TGS. The card had bright-colored flowers and the words "Best wishes on Diwali" the face. The inside of the card read:

We celebrate Diwali with Lights and Crackers. With

lights we Propose to Greet Happiness and with crackers to humor the Devil. Let me wish you success in your mission.

Our children were being taught about the history of India and Africa and celebrating Diwali. What ever happened to George Washington and the Fourth of July?

George Washington and the Fourth of July had as little meaning to Africans and Asians as Diwali had to me. We were living in another culture with different holidays. There were going to be a lot of holidays we found in Africa that were new to us. There was Guy Fawkes Day, which the British celebrated with fireworks. This was to commemorate an attempted bombing of the House of Lords in 1605. Another holiday that was new to us was Boxing Day. This is a bank holiday in England so called for the boxes given to postmen and errand boys on the first weekday after Christmas.

My wife and I wrote to our parents weekly. The children wrote also. Writing was difficult for them. The best they could do was to draw pictures for grandma and grandpa. I thought it might be better to let the kids send a cassette tape recording to their grandparents. They couldn't write, but they could talk. In that way, the children would be able to tell more about what they were doing. One evening just before bedtime the kids made a tape to send to the grandparents in New York. The following is a transcript of the tape.

> (John speaking) Hello. How are you? Good. Ah, This is John. Ah, I can't tell anything. (At this point I coached him on what to say.) I have a nice time. I have my friends. Ah, Douglas and David. Ah, I don't wet my pants anymore. I don't wear diapers at night. I am a big boy. I go in Kenner garder, in Janewarie, Jainer, Jani—I can't say it.

Jenreru, I can't—(I coach here.) January. Are you going to come and visit at us? It's easy, just gotta get on the airplane and they bre, ah they bring you right over. Then we will come and get her. She has to have shots first. Be good. SMMAAKK!! That was a big kiss. Goodbye.

(Paula speaking) Hello Grandpa and Gramma. We are having a nice time here. Ah, at school we have to wear a certain kind of dress—green and white checked dress. Ah, we're having a good time. We're having a play at school. It's called *Hansel and Gretel.* Ninos is Gretel. She's an Indian girl at our class. Anthony is Hansel, and he's a boy at our school—African. I am the Stepmother. There is a boy called Manish, he's the father. Stephen is a tree, and all the rest are trees. Winnie is the girl, and she's the narrator. There's another play called—I don't know the name, but it's Jesus when he was borned, and Beth is an angel. And there's Tico and Fifi and they are angels. Helen is Mary, and a book is the baby. There is a lady called Miss Roop: and we went there to have dinner, and all the people came. Goodbye. "Give her a big kiss!" John shouted at the end of Paula's letter/tape home.

(Beth speaking) This is Beth, Grandma and Grampa. We made up some plays at our school, and Douglas is the woodcutter. We have a paw-paw tree in our yard, and the Gatchell's paw-paw tree fell down when it was real stormy. We climbed on it. We went to Mbale, and Sheva is a girl at Tororo Girls school, and we went to her house, and her father gave us some ice cream." (Sheva is an Indian girl who was a TGS student.) "Bye."

(John again) Hello. How are you? Good. I have some friends—Douglas and David. And Douglas is David's friend and David is Douglas's friend. I have a nice time and I am a big boy that I didn't wet my new sheets: and I have a new colored bed spread. I do. And, I am a big boy. SSMMAAKK! There's a big kiss. Goodbye.

John was really getting into it now. He kept interrupting the other kids and had a lot of big kisses to send.

(Stephen speaking) This is Stephen. Tell everyone I said "Hello." I wonder how your weather is and if you have had any bad storms. If you get any American stamps, could you send them to me in an envelope? Goodbye. (Stephen was collecting stamps and could trade American stamps with the African and Asian children.)

(Paula again) I saw Stephen jump off the diving board at the swimming pool, and there is a little pool John plays in. We went in with Gatchells, and John rode in Douglas' balloon boat. There is a little slide in the little pool, and we go down the little slide on our stomachs. We pretend that we are alligators and go after the little kids. The big pool has a big slide. I went down the big slide, but I got water up my nose. I didn't want to slide down it anymore because it was too much of a splash.

(Beth again) At the pool there is monkeys in the trees and baboons, and apes. (I don't know where Beth got "apes" from. There are no apes in Uganda. Apes are in the Congo, not Uganda or Kenya.) There are great big beetles as big as daddy's glasses, his eye glass, the glass in his glasses. There is this girl at Tororo Girls School called Eujennie, and she caught it for us and it made a noise like this, EEEKKK! But we got it and flushed it down the toilet. The Africans catch them and eat them. Goodbye.

At this point, it was bedtime so the kids sang some Sunday school songs to their grandparents and said "goodnight."

The Patels invited the Andrezejewskis, the Gatchells, and Joyce and me to their Diwali dinner. The Patels lived in downtown Tororo on the second floor of one of the stores on the main street. We were invited for dinner at 8 p.m. When we arrived, the apartment had a delicious curry smell. The Indian food we were served was very much like a Mexican buffet; consisting of some kind of a spicy soup, chicken curry served over rice, and sweet rice cakes. The Asians do not drink or serve alcohol and do not eat pork. "Oh, no, we don't eat piggy," as Mr. Patel would say.

What I remember most about the meal was that the inside of the Patel home was very dark. The only lights that I recall were candles and oil lamps. The other unusual thing was that only the men ate with the guests. There were three Asian men and their wives there that evening. While we were eating in the dining room, I could see through a doorway that the three Asian wives were sitting on the kitchen floor eating their meal. We were not introduced to the wives. I had never seen these women before and never remember seeing them after that night. They were preparing the food that was served by African servants to their husbands and guests. As we were eating, I could hear these Asian wives giggling from time to time. When I passed by the kitchen on the way out, these women turned their heads and covered their faces with veils. I suppose that the way the three American wives were treated seemed as strange to our hosts as the way the Asian wives were treated seemed to us.

The Patels must have been wealthy. They owned several of the buildings in Tororo and had been in business for several years. However, the Patel home did not show any indication of affluence. It may have been that the Asian people knew that the Africans would deport them and take their homes. This is just what happened a few years after I left Uganda. The Asians were put on airplanes and sent to England with only the clothing they were wearing.

I had to do something about our children's education. We would be returning to the States in two-years' time, and I did not want them to fall behind their American peers. I had heard about an American correspondence course that some missionary families were using. It is called The Calvert School. So, I wrote for information regarding these courses.

9

"A woman in my village gave birth to a river, and every time she comes to the river it opens for her to let her pass on dry land." A student is talking to me. Now, this is a third-year student. This is an educated 17-year-old African girl saying this.

What are you talking about? I think. This is stupid. Do I look that dumb? A woman gives birth to a river. I hold my hand on my chin and looking the girl directly in the eye say, "How can that be? Women don't give birth to rivers. Rivers don't open for people to cross." This girl is serious. She says, "What about Moses and the Red Sea? Do you believe that the Red Sea opened for Moses to cross with the children of Israel?" She has me. I am taught to believe this. "Well, I guess I do." "Well then," she continues, "Why don't you believe me? A woman in my village gave birth to a river, and it opens for her to cross."

"A woman in my village gave birth to a python, and she plays with it." That is another story a student tells me. "A woman in my village gave birth to a leopard. It is black and white and it is our brother," another student. I find these stories impossible to believe, and say so.

One day an African man knocks at my door and says, "I am told you don't believe that a man in my village can change into a leopard. I am here to take you to my village, and he will change into a leopard before your eyes." I decline. "No, I am not going to travel to your village to see a man change into a leopard. I'll pass on that one."

"I am the woman who has brought the rains." This is an African woman on the main street of Tororo. She is dancing around me in the street, yelling in her tribal language. An Asian shop-keeper is translating for me. "She says, that you look well-bathed, clean, and well-fed. Now, she wants you to pay her for bringing the rain." I give the woman a shilling, and she did a chanting dance around the children and me. "What does that woman want?" Paula asks. "She claims she has brought us rain so we can take showers, Paula," I reply. Paula looks at the woman. I pass by with the children and say, "Just come with me and ignore her, maybe she'll go away." We pass on.

What kind of a life have I gotten myself and family into? Women give birth to rivers, leopards. Other women bring rains. What kind of a place is this? Am I sane? Do women give birth to something other than babies?

The space program. We want to have a man on the moon within ten years. The Sikhs have already done that according to Didi Bawa, but it didn't cost so much money. Didi Bawa is the Asian travel agent in Tororo, and he claims that some Sikh has already been on the moon, but it was cheaper for the Sikhs to go there. Probably government graft. Americans always pay too much. Ask Didi Bawa. He knows about the price of going to the moon. After all, he's the travel agent.

This place is crazy. I am crazy for coming here. I want to be back in New York. The *Uganda Argus,* the only newspaper in Uganda, carries articles about rain stoppers, bewitching, and witch craft. In this culture even the educated believe in this sort of thing.

BUGERERE THREAT

Kezekia Mukasa, of Keyunga, Bugerere, has received a letter threatening that he will be killed for allegedly stopping the rain in the area.

Mukasa has reported the matter to the acting Gombolola chief, Mr. Nuwa Damba, who told him that it will be investigated.

A man alleged to be a rain stopper has been killed at Kangulumira, Bugerere.

BEWITCHED

Sipriamo Tusimule, seven, is alleged to have been cut to death by Katabazi, thirty, cultivator at Nyarurambi village. Katabazi alleged that Tusimulel's father had bewitched him.

TAXING WITCH DOCTORS

Our country needs a lot of money for economic development. It is important that all people who earn income contribute through the payment of taxes.

Unfortunately, there is a group of income-earners which is apparently being ignored.

These are the witch doctors. To be more specific, the female witch doctors, although even the male ones are not taxed according to their income earnings.

The number of such people, especially in rural areas, is quite high in this country.

Some of them are helpful; others worse than useless. But one thing they have in common is that they all get a great deal of money out of the masses.

May the authorities concerned bring all the witch doctors within the net of taxation and tax them according to their income. This will not only have the effect of aiding our country's economic growth, but will also discourage false witch doctors. Thereby, cutting down the exploitation of the masses.

There is a wire fence between Bill Gatchell's house and ours. The fence ends at a five-foot hedge. I have Onyango dig up some of the hedge at the end of the fence so I can have easier access to Bill Gatchell's door. Now I don't have to walk out my driveway and up the road and down Gatchell's driveway to his door. I simply walk around the end of the fence through the hole in the hedge and across his lawn. Bill Gatchell sees the hole in his hedge, and he is angry. He is furious! "Planting hedges in Africa is like planting ideas," he says, "If the Africans don't destroy them, the Europeans will dig them up." That's true. I have dug up his hedge. I assumed it was a small price to pay for my company, apparently, it was not.

The Cambridge examinations are coming. This year our students will take the Cambridge Overseas Examinations. We need to have our students do well. It is the reason for TGS. The girls must do well on the Cambridge. Who can help us prepare our students for the British Cambridge Overseas examinations? The British can help us.

Bill and I travel to Kampala to a British secondary school for help with the Cambridge. We want them to help us prepare our students for this examination. This British school has been in Uganda for years and has had a good record with the Cambridge. So, we need their advice and help—copies of previous examinations, advice as to what we should be teaching. We're new at this, and we need guidance.

Forget it. The British are not going to help. After a

day with these people, we are more confused than before. We are "Yanks" not British. They tell us that we have no business being in Uganda. After all, "It is part of the former British Colonial Republic, isn't it?" and "Who do we think we are trying to teach American ways to British subjects?" All I can do is shake my head and wonder just why we're here. The British certainly don't want us here and will do all they can to see that we fail miserably. What do we do now? I thought the British were our friends. I have an uncle who flew a B-17 in England to protect their country. How many Americans died protecting dear old England? My grandparents came to the States from England. We're supposed to be friends, even if I don't like tea.

Shocked, Bill Gatchell and I ride back from Kampala and the meeting with our British allies. They don't want TGS to be successful. Tororo Girls School is a threat to them. They don't like us. How many times have we, Americans, helped them? Now, just once they could help us. Do they? Forget it. We're not their friends here. "Planting ideas in Africa is like planting bushes. If the Africans don't destroy them, the Europeans will dig them up." Gatchell is right.

USAID wants good results on the Cambridge, and the United States Ambassador wants good results on the Cambridge. A lot of money has been put into the Tororo Project. Now it is time to collect in the form of a high-pass percentage on the Cambridge examinations—expensive plant and equipment, expensive faculty. How can TGS go wrong? USAID wants results.

No one ever told me about the Cambridge Overseas Examinations. I have no experience with this test. I don't really care. I am here to teach. My job is to help students learn to type, to write shorthand, and to have some knowledge about business. I don't do Cambridge. I don't know anything about it. Go talk to the British. They do Cambridge. This Uganda mess is their doing. They made Milton Obote the vice president. Go talk to Milton.

    Day by day I teach my classes and something is happening. African girls who had never seen a typewriter before they walked into my classroom are starting to type. They are typing letters. They are typing manuscripts. They are increasing typing speed and accuracy. They can even type tables of numerical information in columns that are neatly placed on a page. They are taking dictation in shorthand, and are able to give me a typewritten transcript that is 95 percent accurate. These girls who have never seen a department store are able to understand how things work. They know about lines of communication and lines of authority. Someday the British will be out of this former colony and my "girls" will be doing the job. They will type letters, they will take shorthand, they will be able to do the job. Who cares about the Cambridge? The British can keep their Cambridge examination. It is not needed here. We are doing fine without it. God Save the Queen and all that other "bloody" garbage. We can do it without you, dear old England. The Yanks have landed.

10

The African secretary at TGS called to me as I was walking past the office saying, "Mr. Stewart, your car and sea freight have arrived. You may pick them up at the train station in Tororo."

At last! A car. For the past several weeks I had been dependent upon other staff for transportation to and from town. Now I will be able to drive myself. What a feeling of freedom this gave us! We could take the kids to school, go to the grocery store, to the post office, or even just take a ride if we wanted.

George and I drove the TGS truck to the train depot, and there it was. My beautiful car! My blue and white VW station wagon waiting for me to drive away. Wow! Did that look good. As we walked into the station I saw the wooden boxes with my name stenciled on the side.

William D. Stewart
Tororo Girls School
Tororo, Uganda
EAST AFRICA

After the pages and pages of forms had been filled out and the boxes loaded into the TGS truck, I put the keys in the ignition and "ROARR!!!" I was off. As I followed the TGS truck back to the house, I realized that I was on the wrong side of the road. The steering wheel was closer to the side of the road not near the center like in the States. This was going to take some getting used to. Driving was particularly difficult for me at crossroads. It is natural to look in the opposite direction for oncoming cars. It was like learning to drive all over again. One American made this mistake and his daughter was killed in an accident the first week he got his car.

We unloaded the boxes at the house, and we all had a good time unpacking the "treasures" we had packed so long ago in New York. The kids were especially happy to unpack their favorite toys, books, and clothing. "Oh, Beth, look at this!" Paula said. John was walking around with his truck in his hand and yelling to the Gatchell children, "We got our sea freight, come and see." The place was starting to look like home at last. Our dishes, our blankets, our books, our trucks, and dolls, and clothes. Now we had more than just a vacation's worth of clothes to wear. Best of all—our car! New York State license plates. These had to go. I applied for car registration, was given a number, and had to take it to a tinsmith to make up license plates—black and white.

Now we could do something, we could go some place. For weeks we had been just sitting around the house with no way to get out and see Uganda. Now, we could do something, anything. We still had not seen elephants, lions, zebras, giraffe.

My thoughts went back to the day we had been at Entebbe airport and passed through Kampala. I remembered crossing Owen Falls Dam and lunch with Mary Riley at Jinja on the shore of Lake Victoria. I remembered, also, how sick I had felt, how depressed I had been. Those were not good memories. Now we could replace those memories with better times.

It had taken us almost three months to get over the

initial "culture shock" that newcomers experience. Now, the depression had been replaced by a curiosity of what was around us. I wanted to see more of Africa than Tororo had to offer.

That month we had a three-day holiday for Ugandan independence, so we decided to take advantage of the new "mobility" our car gave us to visit Kampala, the country's biggest city. We left early Saturday morning and drove our car down that same road we had traveled from Kampala to Tororo. There were two hotels in Kampala. The Grand Hotel is the old, British hotel in the center of town. There is a newer Hilton Hotel, located on a hill overlooking the city. It is called the "Milton Hilton" by Europeans living in Uganda. "Milton" being a reference to the Ugandan President, Milton Obote.

We were told by the others at TGS to stay at the Grand Hotel. The Hilton is modern, but was not yet finished. The rooms were partially done, and the elevators did not work. It was more inconvenient. The Grand Hotel is a comfortable, three-story building with a luxurious grace and charm.

We all got in the car at 9 a.m. and started off. It was a slow trip. I was not used to driving on the British side of the road, and we had taken our camera. We took pictures of the sugarcane, pictures of the banana trees, pictures of Owen Falls Dam and rainbow, pictures of Lake Victoria, pictures of people walking along the road—women with pots on their heads, men with baskets of live chickens, and for John, pictures of goats! goats!

Kampala is a mecca for American, British, French, and German tourists. From the Grand Hotel in Kampala vans of tourists were coming and going from the airport and to and from the game lodges. The hotel is on a corner. The first floor is the registration lobby and gift shops. Up just one flight of stairs is a large open-air restaurant which overlooks the street corner. Across the street is a park which filled a city block. In this park African craftsmen were selling wood carvings of every description. The biggest selling item was African animals—elephants, lions, etc. There were carvings of African people, and also of fish. In addition to the wood carvers, there were Africans selling paintings, gold, silver, and copper jewelry, bead work, ostrich eggs, safari-type clothing, hats—just about everything one could imagine. It is delightful to sit in this open-air restaurant and watch the people on the street below and across the street in the park. We had a cup of coffee, the children had soft drinks, while we watched the activity. The kids all wanted to buy some of the carvings, and so did Joyce and I. We deposited our suitcases in our room and went out into the crowd to collect some African treasures. We walked through the park and back across the street by the hotel enjoying the warm sunny day and looking at all the unusual items for sale.

We all felt so happy being in Kampala. I believe that it was as though we did not live there. It was as though our liner had stopped at an exotic port of call. We could forget that we lived in Tororo. We were with other tourists. It was almost like being home. What a privilege to be able to do this.

We were ready for Kampala. The others at TGS had told us what to do and where to go in Kampala. First of all, don't take the first price that is given on anything. You have to bargain for prices. Every purchase is like buying a used car. "How much is this?" "Twenty-five shillings?" "What? Do you think I would pay twenty-five shillings for this?" Then you put the item down and turn around to walk away. The vendor says, "How much you give me for this?" You offer some ridiculous figure. "I will give you five shillings." The vendor says, "Five shillings? This is worth more than five shillings. You take this for twenty." He places the item in your hand. You say; "Twenty shillings? Why, I can buy one right down the street for seven shillings." The vendor says, "Where you buy this for seven shillings? You say, "Right back there in the park a man is selling this same item for seven shillings." That's a lie. You know it, and the vendor knows it. "OK" he says, "I give to you for fifteen shillings." You say, "Here," and place a ten-shilling note in his hand, "I'll pay you ten shillings, Na jua Bwana? Sasa mimi nakwenda Tororo." (You understand, Sir. Now, I am going to Tororo.) Now, he knows that you are not a tourist. You know the language, and are not stupid enough to pay his asking price. So, he says, "Asanti sana, Bwana Kubwa." (Thank you very much, Sir.) and he takes the ten shillings and gives you the item. You walk away smiling. Just down the street you see a man selling the same item for less than ten shillings. Then, you don't feel like "Bwana Kubwa."

"Bwana Kubwa." All Europeans are Bwana Kubwa in East Africa. The literal translation of "Bwan" is "Lord" like the British title Lord somebody or other. "Kubwa" means "big." These two words together translate "Lord Big." The Swahili equivalent of "The Big Cheese," I guess. Africans always call white men "Bwana Kubwa." The only time you are not called "Bwana Kubwa." is when you are being addressed by an educated African. They see the European as an equal. But, in the eyes of uneducated Africans you are "The Big Lord."

George Andrezejewski and I used to call each other "Guano Kubwa." substituting for the Swahili "Bwana" the sound-alike English word, "guano." The Swahili word for "Hello" is "Jambo." George and I would shout across the room to each other "Jambo Guano Kubwa," or "Hello, you big bird shit!"

We had been told by the TGS staff that there was a terrific Chinese restaurant in Kampala. It was just up the street from the hotel, so we had dinner there. As we walked up the street to the restaurant we passed by a tree filled with fruit bats. These bats were hanging upside down on every branch of the tree. There must have been hundreds of these crow-sized bats. The activity of the people passing by on the street did not bother these big bats at all. None of them stirred. We had never seen so many bats at one time. They looked like grey, furry fruit hanging from the branches. Later in the evening, the tree was empty.

I enjoy Chinese cooking and was not disappointed. The food we had in this restaurant was one of the finest Chinese meals I have ever had. From then on we made it a point to have at least one meal at this restaurant when we were in Kampala.

The next day we were out early walking along the streets, looking at the stores. There were a lot of shops that sold nothing but tourist items. There were wood carvings, and paintings—much of the same kind of items that were sold in the open-air market. The prices were much higher, but the workmanship was of a better quality. There were also a lot of camera shops. These sold camera equipment, shortwave radios. and tape recorders. I don't remember seeing television sets for sale. Television was not available in Uganda when we were there.

We were looking in one store window filled with leather goods, when we heard several people cry out "Mawevi, Mawevi!" (Thief! Thief!). Suddenly everyone was running down the street chasing an African man. Clerks in stores left their counters and joined in the chase. The African man was quickly surrounded by men and women who were screaming and hitting him. He fell to the sidewalk and the crowd started kicking him. The African man lay still on the sidewalk, and the kicking stopped. The children were scared and were clutching at my legs. John wanted to be held. It was a frightening sight. There were two policemen standing by us watching this beating. I asked them why this man had been beaten. They did not seem upset at all. One of the policemen said, "This man must be beaten, he is a thief. Thieves must be beaten." Stephen asked me "Dad, why was the man kicked?" "That's what Africans do to people who steal," I answered.

I don't know what happened to the man lying on the sidewalk. We went back to the hotel. It felt safer to be with the tourists.

Witnessing the way Ugandans dealt with thieves, one had to bear in mind that this was a different culture. There were always articles in the *Uganda Argus* about thieves being beaten and killed.

Here are just a few:

> An unidentified man was chased and beaten to death after he was accused of breaking into a house and stealing property at Kibwa, near Mutundwe near Kampala. After an alarm was raised, a crowd overpowered the man at Mile 5 on the old Masaka Road, near Natete, and left him dead on the road.

> Lebaleba, aged about 60, of unknown address, was beaten to death by villagers of Kabula-Muliro, Singo, who alleged they had caught him stealing a chicken at night.

> George Wanlera, aged 21, of Kitintale village, Gombolola, was taken to Mulango Hospital under police

escort after he had been beaten by a group of people who accused him of stealing at night.

It is alleged that a Mutongole chief led a gang of villagers at Kiwawa, Bugerere in an attack on Laurence Okoth, 60, and Valantino Owori, 30, whom they believed to be thieves. The men were murdered and their bodies thrown in the River Nile.

Two men were reported by police yesterday to have been beaten to death by villagers on suspicion that they were thieves. Apolo Skitoleko was beaten to death at Kikoiro village for being suspected of stealing 150 shillings, and at Nakakonge, Kamwagi, 35, was beaten to death on suspicion that he had stolen 310 shillings.

Recently, a certain man was beaten to death in front of a certain grocers at Mengo. I understand the man died before dawn, but I was taken aback when I witnessed the sad spectacle at 2 p. m. In fact, the body had already started stinking. There was a swarm of hungry flies over it, and a dog was seen sniffing at the corpse.

Anyway, I am wondering what action the police were taking at the time. It would take time to convince me that the removal of the body was delayed as a result of the investigations taking place at that time. The City Council is also to blame, because it is always its duty to observe sanitary rules.

Actually, this was a shame to our country. Many a tourist may have, after seeing that corpse, conceived a bad impression about Uganda. Worse still, the stinking body was lying in front of a grocers and this may have impregnated some customers with prejudice against the goods.

Lastly, I would like to suggest that it is high time that

we accorded respect to the dead. James Matsiko. Kampala.

There were different rules by which the Ugandan society conducted itself. It was not too long ago that my own ancestors cut off the tongues of liars, gouged out the eyes of Peeping Toms, and cut off thieves' hands. In Uganda thieves are beaten. That is just the way it is. We were Americans and guests in this country. We were not there to change the rules of Ugandan society. In some ways, living in Uganda was like leaving the civilized world and going back to the dark ages.

Tororo was hard to take after visiting Kampala. But, now I had a car and there would be a lot more visits, not only to Kampala, but Nairobi, the Kenyan seashore, and game parks—the elephants, lions, zebras, the giraffes, and goats, goats!

11

Every day in Tororo is warm and sunny. There is a dry season from December to March. The rains come in April and May, and again in September and October. In the rainy season, the days start out with a bright sunrise at 7 a.m. Through the morning, the clouds start to rise off to the west over Lake Victoria and pass east over Tororo. The clouds pass on east to Mount Elgon in Kenya, and it starts to rain. Then this rain travels west back over Tororo again going back toward Lake Victoria. It is always the same. Clouds rising over Lake Victoria, traveling east to Mount Elgon, and coming back with rain to Lake Victoria. We got these rains in the late afternoon for an hour or so. So, most of the days were sun filled, even during the rainy season. Because Uganda is on the equator, the sunrise is at 7 a.m. and sundown is at 7 p.m. The days are never longer or shorter.

We got up with the sun, got dressed, and Francis had breakfast waiting for us. The kids liked an East African breakfast of Posho. Posho is a cooked cereal much like Cream of Wheat and is produced in Uganda. We could get American-type cereal, but it was never very good. This American-type cereal is produced in Britain and shipped to Africa. By the time the cereal reaches East Africa from Britain, it is stale.

Once, our Rice Krispies cereal box had a contest picture on the back panel. The object of the contest was to find as many animals as you could in a jungle of lines. Every morning the kids would write down the kinds of animals they found. When they had their lists complete, they wanted to send them in for the contest. As we were reading the fine print for an address, we found that the contest had expired almost a year before. That cereal was over a year old when we bought it from Tororo General!

Posho doesn't come in a nice box and doesn't have contests with prizes, but it is fresh. The problem with Posho is worms. The cereal comes in a paper bag, much like pancake mix. However, it becomes wormy very quickly. In fact, some Posho had worms in it when we opened it up. I gave up taking wormy Posho back to Tororo General. We just told Francis to sift the Posho, and remove the worms. A British family told us we were too fussy. They just cooked the cereal worms and all.

After a breakfast of wormy Posho or stale Rice Krispies, I drove the kids to school. The school was in town about a mile or so from our home. On the way back I would stop at the post office before returning home. Sometimes the mail was already sorted by then, most times I had to wait until noon.

The post office in Tororo is on the main road just out of the center of town. Since the climate is always nice, the post boxes are opened from outside the building. There is a covered porch area on the perimeter of the building. The boxes are on the wall of the building. The postal workers put the mail in the boxes from inside the building, and the public opens the mail boxes on the outside wall. If you want to send mail or purchase stamps, there is an inside lobby.

After I dropped the kids off at their school and picked up the mail, I would return home. John was too young for school. He got up later than the other kids and would be

From my house to Toro Girls School (showing clock/water tower).

directing Francis in the preparation of his breakfast. John would still be in his pajamas whether he was eating breakfast or reading his books. He got dressed later in the day and played with the Gatchells youngest boy, Douglas. Our home was right on the TGS campus, so I was able to walk home between my classes.

In addition to the day classes, the faculty were assigned "duty." Duty consisted of being present at the dining hall for student meals, supervising a study period in the evening, and making sure all students were in bed at 10 p.m. with lights out. "Lights out" was difficult to supervise. There were dormitories for 400 girls divided into rooms containing four beds. African students are used to staying up late at night in the villages talking around bonfires. It is not their habit or desire to get in bed at 10 p.m. I walked around the campus yelling, "All right, you girls, turn off the lights, stop talking, and get to sleep!" When the students were quiet, I walked home. Walking at night in Africa is accomplished by scuffing dirt and small stones ahead of your steps. This alerts snakes of your approach. Scuff, scuff, scuff. Here I come you snakes. Make way for Bwana Kubwa.

During the day, peddlers stopped by the house selling wood carvings, ink drawings, Persian rugs, fruit, and eggs. There is a process for buying eggs. The egg vendors have the eggs wrapped in banana leaves. The eggs are unwrapped and put into a pot of water. If the eggs float, they are not good. Don't buy eggs that float. Then one inspects the eggs to make sure they have not been washed. Don't buy clean eggs. A Peace Corps doctor warned me about this. When a chicken lays an egg, nature puts a protective film over the egg. Washing the egg removes this film, and virus can invade the egg shell. The eggs in our refrigerator always looked dirty. Just the way we like them. Dirty and virus free.

After the floaters and clean eggs are removed, you have to bargain for price. Even after months of buying eggs from the same vendor, the price still had to be bargained. The eggs we bought at the door in Tororo were smaller than eggs purchased in the States and had yolks that were a dark orange color.

The eggs are inferior in quality to those purchased in America, but the fruit is fantastic. The oranges are yellow and green, but very nice tasting. African bananas are smaller, but taste much sweeter than those purchased in the States. Pineapples have to be tested. One pulls out one of the green spears from the top of the pineapple. If it comes out easily, it's ripe and ready to eat. If it's hard to pull out, the fruit has been picked too soon and is not ripe.

After dinner we spent a lot of our spare time visiting neighbors. Someone had always just returned from some trip to Kenya, one of the game parks, or Europe. At the end of the year, our contract provided airfare to Europe to get away from our primitive surroundings. Sort of an R&R (rest and relaxation). Most of the staff took pictures of their trips with 35 mm slide film. In the evenings we would all look at the pictures via slide projection.

We had come to Uganda on a direct flight from Newark Airport and had not seen anything of the world. By the end of our two-year tour, we would have seen Egypt, Greece, Italy, France, Germany, Denmark, Sweden, Norway, Holland, Belgium, England, Scotland, and the game parks in Kenya and Uganda. We would have ridden on everything from airplanes to camels. I prefer airplanes.

Someone would say, "Hey, Bill, bring your family over after dinner, and look at our trip to Israel." "Great," I would reply. "See you about eight." "Hey, Bill" Gatchell would yell across the yard, "We got some great slides of Mombasa, come on over tonight." Most of the evenings were spent looking at slides, playing chess, or solving the world's problems.

Uganda has a perfect climate for gardening. We had been told by Doubleday to be sure and bring a variety of seeds. The gardening is great, but the seed supply is poor. We brought all kinds of seeds and had a great garden. Being from New York, I was not used to having a long growing season. My prize crop was watermelon. We gave a watermelon to Onyango. He had never seen watermelon. I kept waiting for him to tell me how good it was, but he never mentioned it. Finally, I said, "Onyango, did you like the watermelon I gave you?" He said "It was not good."

Onyango was not noted for his tact. "We cut it up, and boiled it, but it came to nothing. We tasted the soup; but it was not good, and we threw it." I had forgotten to tell him not to cook watermelon.

George was right, and Gatchell was right. George said there are a lot of snakes. He was right. There were a lot of snakes. Gatchell said keep the grass short. He was right. The grass had to be kept short. In addition, Bill gave me a tip about paying the "shamba man" (garden or outside man) for dead snakes. We paid Onyango 15 bob for every snake he killed in the yard. Whenever a snake appeared in the hedge, drainage ditch, or in a tree, I called Onyango. "Onyango, nakuja hapa pasi sona. Eko nyoka hapa." (Onyango, come here quickly. There is a snake here.)

I saw a bright green snake in the hedge and called Onyango. He came over, saw the snake, and said "Hapana, bwana, eko kali mingi." (No, sir, that is a mean snake.) We shook that one out of the hedge with a garden rake and killed it with the slasher. It was one of those "three steppers" George had warned me about.

Bill Gatchell and I were talking in his living room one day when Carl, Bill's 9-year-old came in and said, "Dad, Douglas has a huge centipede." "OK" Bill said, not wanting to be distracted from what he was telling me. A short time later Carl came in again and said, "Dad, Douglas' centipede is REALLY BIG!!" Bill turned to his son and said, "Carl don't bother me now, I am talking to Mr. Stewart." "But Dad," Carl said, "This is the biggest centipede I have ever seen!" Now, Carl had our interest. He had seen a lot of centipedes in the last year. "How big is it?" Bill asked. Holding his hands about a foot apart Carl said, "This Big!" "Douglas!" Bill yelled, "Get away from that centipede!" Bill and I hurried out to the porch and there was Douglas playing with a black snake. I don't know if it was poisonous. Bill killed the snake and gave Douglas a warning about playing with big centipedes.

There were a lot of "snake tales" in Uganda. One evening the Headmistress, Phyllis Roop, went to bed and turned out the light. In the darkness she heard a "splat" sound. Phyllis said she was tired and tried to forget the sound and go to sleep, but could not. She reached over to the bedside stand, and turned on the light. There on her polished cement floor was a cobra.

How about the biology teacher? She was sitting in her living room looking through the sliding glass doors when a black mamba "kali mingi!" (very mean) slid under the sliding glass door and on to her living room floor. She said she wanted it for a specimen, and tried to kill it with insecticide. After two cans of East African "DUDU KUFU" (dead bug) the snake lay dazed on the floor. She picked it up with salad tongs and put it into a jar. One evening during the rainy season I was reading in our living room. It was late, and the children were in bed. As I sat in the quiet of the room, I heard a sound "HISS!" I looked up, puzzled by the sound. Then I heard it again, "HISS!" I started looking around the room without moving. There was a snake somewhere in the room. "HISS!" I knew that sound was coming from this room. "HISS!" It was close. In this room. But, where? I looked around the foot of my chair. Nothing. I stood up. "HISS!" Where was that snake? I carefully started removing everything from the room. Piece by piece the furniture was removed. The cushions from the chairs and sofa were removed. The slasher was in my hand ready for the attack. The room was empty now. "HISS!" The curtains! The cobra was in the curtains. I shook the curtains. No snake. I removed the curtains. No snake. "HISS!" The room was bare. No

A cobra I killed in my yard. Bill Gatchel feigns fear and my daughter Paula watches.

furniture, no curtains, just the cement floor and walls. "HISS!" It was coming from the center of the room. "HISS!" I walked over to the center of the room and stood underneath the ceiling light. "HISS!" Oh, how stupid. What an idiot. It was the rainy season and the flat cement roof was dripping water on the hot electric bulb in the ceiling light. "HISS!"

We had a snakebite kit in our refrigerator. It consisted of three syringes filled with liquid. The first two were to counteract the snake venom, and the third was to counteract the first two should an allergic reaction occur. If you were at death's door it would probably "pull you through." I'm glad we never had to use it.

12

Mr. John Okoch, a teacher at East Sare Central School, Cherangani, Kitale, was on Tuesday attacked in the school compound by a group of about ten people who started to circumcise him.

It is understood the group escaped before completing the operation when friends of Mr. Okoch came to his rescue from a nearby village. They found Mr. Okoch bleeding and took him to the district Commissioner's office, then to Kitale District Hospital for completing of the circumcision operation. Mr. Okoch, 26, from Samia Location is understood to have been teaching in the area for many years. According to his tribe, he is not liable for circumcision."

"Bill," I said, walking in the door of Gatchell's house, "Look at this article in the *Uganda Argus*. An African teacher was attacked at his school, and some men tried to circumcise him." "Well," Gatchell replied, "that's no skin off my back, or anywhere else." "No." I insisted, "This really happened—circumcised!" "It's that time of year," Bill replied.

I asked the students in my typewriting class to write a short story about their village. This gave the girls practice with English composition, helped their typing skills, and gave me an insight into tribal customs. Juliet Osire wrote about circumcision.

Circumcision in Bugisu takes place after every two years.

Only men are circumcised and if at all any of them is not circumcised, he is considered an outsider and he is not at all respected.

Before circumcision, all small boys and men who have not been circumcised gather together and call all their relatives including their girlfriends so that they dance from door to door or from village to village. If they chance to dance on your compound, you must give them a present usually a goat or a hen; otherwise, they won't move away.

All the dancers dress very typically. They dress in banana leaves, and paint themselves white with powder. A person who is to be circumcised puts on beads, bird's feathers, and bells so that he will be recognized. The dancing usually goes on for about one or two months.

The day before the ceremony is to take place, dancing must go on with lively music and drumming until dawn. This is a day when a boy is expected to get many presents. Some might even get ten goats and a number of hens.

On the day of circumcision which is usually done in the evenings, a boy must not shake or show any signs of fear. If he does, he is considered a coward. Only specialized people perform this ceremony. Always when a boy is sick after the ceremony, his girlfriend is not to see him because the sight of girls is believed to increase pain.

We were on the edge of the Bugisu tribal area and were hearing a lot about circumcision. The young men who are candidates for circumcision are between 16- and 20-years-old.

Circumcision to the Bugisu tribe is considered very important and treated with the same enthusiasm as Christmas in the States. The Bugisu girls at Tororo Girls School were excited about circumcision and were talking about their brothers' circumcisions, their boyfriends' circumcisions, and their friends' circumcisions.

We saw groups of young men dancing and yelling on

Candidates going to relatives' and friends' homes where they dance and receive circumcision gifts.

the road. The circumcision candidate is dressed in feathers, has his face painted white, and is usually wearing some kind of animal skin. There are drums, spears, chanting, and dancing as these groups of young men dance down the road.

The TGS girls told our children how wonderful circumcision was and about the gifts given to those who were to be circumcised. "Dad," Paula asked, "What's circumcision?" We were driving into Tororo and had just passed a group of young men in tribal dress, beating drums, and brandishing spears. "Well," I said to the kids, "It is hard to explain what circumcision is, but I'll show you when we get to town." As we neared the town, there were some tribal-looking men talking at the side of the road. I pulled the car over and said to the kids; "Now, see that man's penis? He's circumcised. Now, look at the man dressed in feathers. He's not circumcised. See the difference?" "No." Paula said. I reached in my shirt pocket, took out a pencil, and drew a picture of the difference on a piece of notepad paper for the kids to examine. The kids looked at the drawing and then back at the group of Africans talking across the road. "Oh! I see," said Beth. She took the notepad from me and explained to Paula. Stephen didn't say anything. I couldn't tell if he was embarrassed, angry, or just not interested. That settled the circumcision curiosity with the kids. They had seen it and knew what it was. No big deal. So what?

The spectacle of naked people is natural in Africa. The "naked" women usually wear a loin cloth, exposing only the breasts; but "naked" African men wear only sandals (usually made from sections of car tires) and, in some areas, a headdress. People are clothed in the larger cities like Kampala and Entebbe, but we were a long way from Kampala and we did see naked people from time to time. One of the most common sights is African women breast-feeding their babies. Without bras the breasts become elongated. I have seen women washing clothes in a stream with breasts tied back to keep them from getting in the way of the washing. I have also seen women walking down the road with a baby on their back and a breast being pulled back over the woman's shoulder by the child to nurse on. Another common sight is naked children. Again, though, the girls usually wear a loincloth.

There were two extremes. The *Uganda Argus* carried the following story under the headline:

KAMPALA MOB ATTACKS "MINI" GIRLS

About 15 girls wearing mini-dresses were attacked by over 50 men at the South Street taxi park, Kampala on Saturday. Some of them had their clothing torn off. The "mini war" started about 2:30 p.m. when some of the men in the gang started questioning girls on whether they wanted to go naked, as they were wearing minis. The first three girls who were attacked said that in Uganda people were allowed to wear what they liked and had their own choice. After this the gang started tearing the girls' clothing, telling them that if they wanted to go naked they should tell the public about it.

This happened in Kampala, where nakedness is thought of as being primitive. We were located over 100 miles from Kampala, and the sight of naked people was not unusual. To the north of us, in the Karamoja section of Uganda, most of the people are naked. Again, however, the women do wear a loincloth.

Karamoja is a desert area. The only town, Moroto, consists of a gas station, a police station, and a small general store.

The Karamojong people are war-like carrying spears and wrist knives. Wrist knives are bracelets with a sharp blade. These people don't grow crops, but, live on a mixture of milk and cow's blood. The Karamojong area is the most primitive spot I have ever been in. The men wear sandals and have a headpiece. This headpiece is woven hair from the man's ancestors. When a man dies, his hair is added to the headpiece and is worn by the son. The skin under the lower lip is pierced and a plug is inserted into the hole. The Karamojong women wear necklaces of colored beads. They have several of these bead necklaces going from just under the chin to the top of the shoulders.

Karamajon man with head piece of ancestors' hair and metal plug under his lower lip.

The entire neck is covered with beads. When the woman is married, the beads are taken off and replaced with coils of thick wire.

We drove to Karamoja. It is a trip of a little over one hundred miles. There is no place to stay, so we had to get in and out in one day. The people allowed us to photograph them for a price. The "going rate" for photographs was a shilling. The Karamojong don't speak English or Swahili. They didn't speak to us, they just used their hands to demand the shilling per photo payment. It is a hot, dusty trip. There is only one unpaved road in Karamoja. The people are interesting to see, but not friendly. I didn't like the trip. The police station had a room full of spears that had been confiscated in cattle wars. We were allowed to purchase some spears to take back with us. The children, especially Stephen and John, liked their spears. This was the beginning of their African "neat things" collection.

The cattle wars in Karamoja are due to "Bride Price." In Karamoja men "purchase" their brides by paying the woman's father with cows. This practice of "bride price" is common to all tribes of this area—the Karamojong, the Turkana, the Jie. They all steal cattle from each other. When the cattle are stolen, the owner is killed.

These cattle wars are reported in the *Uganda Argus:*

> Turkana tribesmen are alleged to have attacked Karamojong at Magor grazing area, Bokora. They stole 460 cattle.
>
> Cattle raiders believed to be Turkana tribesmen armed with rifles and spears attacked Jie tribesmen and took 600 head of cattle. They first raided Lopeci grazing area, Karamoja, where they took 400 cattle; on the same day, at Kanamath, Kotido, they made off with another 200.

These cattle wars have been going on for years, and have caused problems between Uganda and Kenya. It makes the area dangerous to visit. In fact, on the Michelin map of Uganda this is listed as a "forbidden area." Tourists are not allowed to be there.

The Andrezejewskis drove to Karamoja with us. It is not wise to travel alone in this area. The Karamojong men have a custom of cutting a line of puncture wounds around their arms. One circle of little bumps for each man they have killed in a cattle raid; similar to the old gunfighters in the American West who put notches on their guns. I wanted to photograph a Karamojong man who

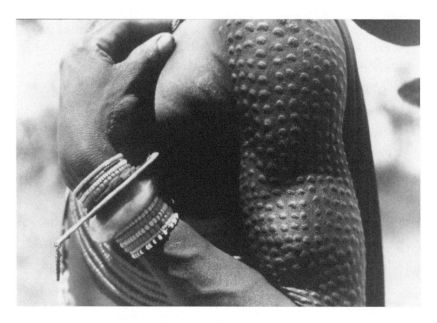

Karamajon man with rings of scars around his arm for each man he has killed in cattle wars for bride price.

was "adorned" from elbow to shoulder on both arms with these "death notches." George said, "You tell him I said He's not so tough." "Very funny, George," I replied, "Tell him yourself—after I'm gone."

Bride price is not restricted to the Karamoja area. Most of the tribes in Uganda buy and sell brides for cows. A woman is worth more if she has a baby before she is married. That way the groom knows the girl is a "producer," and that he will get his bride price back when girls are born. A sort of "security in old age" African style. If a woman doesn't produce children, she can be returned to her father for a bride price refund. The exception to this premarriage child bearing was the students at TGS.

Their parents were paying school fees and wanted the girls to complete secondary education. One of our girls got pregnant and aborted the fetus by putting a stake in the ground, covering it with cow manure, and sitting on it. The tear of her female organs and the resulting infection caused by the cow manure aborted the baby.

The TGS girls brought a high bride price. They would not only bear children, insuring future bride price for their husbands, they would be able to work and make money as well. The cattle wars were avoided in most tribes because of a "time payment" plan. The girl's father did not have to be paid all at once. African men could pay one cow at a time over a period of years.

In the villages, multiple wives were the rule rather than the exception. When a Ugandan man married, it was seldom for love. It was a business transaction. The woman dug his crops, prepared his food, and kept the compound clean. When she had children, she had the added responsibility of child care. Many times a woman would tell her husband, "I have too much work now with the children. You must get another wife to help me." The wife would then bring her younger sister to be the second wife. This second wife shared the work of digging, cooking, and child care. This could go on for three, four, or five wives. In the case of sisters, the relationship of the women was established. This provided a "pecking order" that was present before the women married. The problem with multiple marriage came with wives who were not from the same village. It was very bad when a man's wives were from different tribes. One of the girls at TGS told me that her mother was poisoned by her father's second wife. It was strange to hear girls say, "This girl is my sister—same father different mother."

However, Uganda was changing regarding marriage

customs. The European influence was bringing a "one man, one woman" culture. This was starting in the towns and cities where the exposure to Western ideas was strongest. From time to time, this was seen in the newspaper:

HOT MILK INSTEAD OF HOT WORDS

A Kampala nurse who went to visit her "bachelor" boyfriend is now convalescing from milk scalds.

Entering the house, she was welcomed by a woman—who was the boyfriend's legal wife, although the visitor did not realize this.

The wife told the visitor that the man had gone on safari, but was expected back in a few minutes, and suggested, "Do stay for a cup of tea while you are waiting."

The hostess laid out the cups on the table, and after a few minutes in the kitchen, entered with a large pot of hot milk—which she poured over the visitor's head, causing serious burns.

Fortunately, the bewildered visitor had long hair, which saved her from even more serious harm.

She rushed into the street, chased by the wife who shouted after her, "You will suffer more if you don't leave my husband. Find your own husband instead of looking for other people's."

KNOCK BRINGS HIM A CLOUT

A husband who knocked on the door of his house in Kitisuru Road, Nairobi, was answered with a clout on the head from his wife, a Nairobi court was told yesterday when the wife, Mrs. Pauline Chemelel Henstridge appeared on a charge of assault causing grievous harm.

It is alleged that on September 2, Mrs. Henstridge

struck her husband, Mr. Martin Paul Tindal Henstridge, with an iron bar.

Pleading "Guilty," Mrs. Henstridge said that she struck her husband because "He came home with another woman."

Inspector Z. Luganda told the court that Mrs. Henstridge, an African woman, married her husband, who is a European. For the past three years, there had been trouble in the household, and both had been complaining to the police against each other. The police had advised them to take civil action.

On September 2, when the husband returned home from a walk, he found the house locked on the inside. Mrs. Henstridge refused to open the door.

After persistent knocking, however, she did open it—to strike Mr. Henstridge with an iron bar.

In mitigation she told the court that her husband was with another woman. He tried to beat her (the wife) and then she struck him with the iron bar. The magistrate, Mr. S. Sachdeva, fined Mrs. Henstridge 15 pounds.

The West was having a influence on the towns and cities in Uganda, but Karamoja was a long ways from Kampala—over 400 years, I would guess.

13

The semester was coming to an end, and we would have a month free. The students would be leaving at the end of the week. Typewriting and shorthand classes are easy to grade. I had been giving weekly speed and accuracy tests in these subjects. Shorthand and typewriting grades are not determined by a final examination. The acquisition of a skill is progressive. Students can't cram for shorthand or typewriting finals. Those who practiced typewriting and shorthand during the semester would have built a skill. Introduction to Business, however, is a mental understanding of subject matter that can be measured by an end-of-semester examination. I decided to give a multiple-choice test. If I didn't give a list of possible correct answers, I would end up with answers that made no sense, like "the flag" answer I had gotten earlier.

I gave the test on a Monday so that the students would have the weekend to study. I gave the girls an hour to choose the correct answers of 20 multiple-choice questions. At the end of the class hour, I collected the test papers. That night I graded the tests and returned them the next day.

Before I returned the corrected tests to the students, I told them that I wanted the tests back at the end of class. There was not a lot of material covered in the semester, and I wanted to be able to use this examination with other classes.

I went over each question in the test and gave the students the correct answer. I asked the students if they had any questions about the test. No one spoke. I told the girls to pass their papers to the front of the room. There was still some time left in the class, so the students had to remain seated while I collected and counted the papers.

There were 36 girls in the class, but I had received only 35 test papers back. "Someone didn't hand their paper back," I said. No one said a word. "I need all the test papers. Does someone still have their test paper?" No one spoke. Nothing!

There was one way to get the paper back. "As I call your name, you may leave the room for your next class. Please remain in your seat until your name is called." I said. I started through the papers calling out the name that I found on the test paper. "Euleni Nabwire, Esther Kigundu, May Namirembe, Joyce Akulo, Jacinta Okujaf" ... and on I went until there was just one girl left in the classroom. "Agrippina," I said, "Where's your test paper?" She looked down at her feet and said, "I threw it." I walked over to her and said, "Where did you throw it?" She pointed to the open window. "Out the window? You threw it out the window?" I asked. She shook her head indicating she had. I looked out the window and down on the lawn and sidewalk. "I don't see it." I said. "That's where I threw it. Out the window," she said. "Let's go outside and see if we can find it." I said. We walked down the stairs from the second floor classroom and out to the lawn below the window. "Agrippina," I said, "I don't see your test paper here." She was bent over looking in the grass. "It's here." She held a soft, wet, grey-blue lump of something in her hand. "Here's my paper," she said. I looked at the lump she was holding and asked, "How can that be your paper?" "I ate it." "You ate it? Agrippina, why did you eat your paper?" I asked. She didn't say anything, but I could see she was crying, so I said. "Just go to your next class now, Agrippina." She slowly walked away.

The next day I found a note on my classroom door. It was from Agrippina.

> I am proud because I never got any bad remark except just recently when I did such a silly thing and because I did not want to show it to my teacher who was in charge to see that we were doing well, he took it for granted that I was such a person and this depresses me to death. And I wish I could make him understand that I had no idea in my mind to do anything with the thing I did. Agrippina.

Agrippina was ashamed of her test score and didn't want me ever to see it again, so she chewed it up and threw it out the window.

Maybe it was a cold coming on. I think that we had all gotten something. The kids were irritable, and I was irritable. No one could sleep well. We had all lost our appetite and were depressed. Maybe we were homesick again. When the children started waking up during the night and complaining of stomach pain, I thought it was time to go do a doctor.

Where do you find a doctor? There were three doctors in Tororo. No, there were four. There was a Korean surgeon. Tororo had a hospital and a Korean surgeon, Dr. Kim, worked there. He confined his practice to surgery and was restricted to Ugandan patients by the Ugandan Ministry of Health. Dr. Kim had fled Korea and taken this job in Uganda. His English was very poor.

The other three doctors were British. Two of these three were quite young and treated the British community. The British didn't have anything good to say about them, and the American staff thought they were a joke. The third British doctor was always drunk. He was left over from the old, British colonial days. He lived outside of town somewhere. He came into the bar at the club once in a while. I knew who he was but couldn't depend on him. He was always in the Gin and Tonic and would go off for days at a time. No one seemed to know where he was or when he would come back. So, what do you do for a doctor? I wanted an American doctor. I wanted someone like me. Someone who didn't have an accent to my ears. Someone who had been a Boy Scout, who had gone to the movies and dances in high school, someone who had been to an American college. Someone who ate the things I ate, who had one wife, who had children that looked like my wife and children. Where does one find a doctor like that in Uganda?

"Oh, yes, I know what you mean. Yes, Yes. You can find American doctors like that in Kenya at the African Inland Mission. Just west of Nairobi." An Englishman from Tororo, Roy Godber, was telling me what I wanted to know. "How far is that from here, Roy?" I asked. "You can drive there in about four hours. Have you ever been in Nairobi?" "Never," I said. "Nairobi is very nice, very modern. It would be a wonderful trip for your family to take. Just get on the road in front of your house, and drive four hours east. You'll find all the American doctors you want there. They have a hospital, too."

The Gatchells had been to Nairobi. So had George and his family. Everybody loved Nairobi. "Listen," Bill Gatchell said, "If you liked Kampala, you're going to love Nairobi. When you get there, go to the Fair view Hotel. It's just outside the city and is owned by a British family. The rates are reasonable, the food is good, and it has nice grounds. There are even babysitters for the kids if you want to go into Nairobi in the evening. There are plays, concerts, the whole nine yards; plus, Nairobi Game Park. You drive your car through the park and the animals roam free outside."

"Hey kids," I said when I got home, "do you want to go to Nairobi? We can go see the animals. The elephants, the lions, the giraffe!" They were all excited and jumping around. "Yea! elephants, lions, giraffe. Yea, we want to go to Nairobi!" "John," Paula said, "we're going to see the elephants." "Yes," John said, "and lions too."

We asked the Gatchells to watch our house, told Francis and Onyango that we were going to be gone for a while and to keep coming in and doing their work. If they wanted anything, the Gatchells and Andrezejewskis would be home.

The next morning we packed our luggage, got up with the sun at 7 a.m., and left for African Inland Mission, The Fair View, and Nairobi Game Park.

The Uganda/Kenya border was just about two miles from our home. There was a big log in the road with spikes sticking up to make sure everyone stopped. We pulled up to the border guard, showed him our passports, and told him we were from Tororo Girls School. He directed us around the spiked log, and we were in Kenya.

After the first hour of driving, the countryside changed. At first we saw the usual banana trees, thatch huts, people along the roads with chickens, pots, sugarcane, bananas, and, of course, "goats, goats!" But, we were climbing steadily. Not big hills or mountains, just a gradual rise in elevation. On the left, we passed Mount Elgon, which has an elevation of 14,178 feet. Mount Elgon's claim to fame is the coffee which is grown there. We also passed tea plantations. There are tea leaf pickers dressed in matching red and green garments. This was great stuff! We took pictures of Mount Elgon and of the tea plantation workers gathering tea leaves. The kids didn't seem to be as excited about Mount Elgon and the tea plantations as I did. They wanted to see animals. "Dad!" Stephen said, "When do we see animals?" "Be patient, Stephen!" Paula said, sounding like a mother. I looked in the back at the children. John and Beth were sleeping. Stephen and Paula were awake and complaining about having to ride so far with only tea and Mount Elgon to look at. We reached the town of Eldoret just a little before 9 a.m. Now the air was cooler. My road map of East Africa says that Tororo's elevation is 3,860 feet. Eldoret is listed as 6,870. We had been told to bring sweaters along for the mornings and evenings in Kenya.

Not only had the air changed, the scene around us had also changed. There were very few people on the road, and I had not seen banana trees or thatch huts for miles. After Eldoret the road leveled off to grassland. The land seemed empty. No people, nothing. Just grassland with an occasional tree. Then I saw it! I had to stop the car. The kids had become bored with this grassland view and had turned their attention to their brown paper bags with candy and the usual toys that they always brought along on trips. "Stephen!" I said, pointing off to the right. "Look kids!" "John, John, Wake up." Look at the giraffe." I said, shaking John's leg. Now everyone was looking out the right side of the car. Next to the road was a giraffe that towered above our VW van. It was eating leaves from the top of a tree just next to the road. It didn't seem to be afraid of our car when we stopped. The kids were excited. Our first giraffe. "Wow" Stephen said, "Look at that. John look at the giraffe" "Dad!" Beth said, "Take a picture."

One of the rules of the African road is, "Always bring a camera."

I rolled down the window and took pictures of the giraffe, while the kids threw some of their candy out the windows to feed it. "Don't throw candy out the window. Giraffes don't eat candy." I said. "Hey, Dad," Stephen said, "He's smelling it. The giraffe is smelling the candy." "Stephen, Giraffes don't eat candy. They eat tree leaves. See, he's eating leaves. He doesn't care about your candy." "Well," Stephen said, "he was looking at it." "John." I said, "Don't do that!" "Now, look, Stephen, you have John throwing his bag of candy out the window. Open the door, and get John's candy back. John, the animals don't eat candy. You eat candy. Animals eat other things—leaves!" When Stephen opened the car door and got out to retrieve John's brown paper bag of candy, the giraffe moved off in a slow, jerky kind of a trot away from the car.

14

Eldoret is about one third the distance from Tororo to Nairobi. It is not a "town" but, simply a crossroads. A right turn at Eldoret takes you south through Kenya to Tanzania. Passing eastward brings you to Nairobi.

After Eldoret we started to approach the Rift Valley, and the area where big game is found. As we drove along we passed a sign that said, ELEPHANTS HAVE THE RIGHT OF WAY! "You got that right! I have no problem with that one." I said. It was just after the sign that we saw our first elephant. "WOO! Hey! Kids, look at that, an elephant walking down the road." Everyone crowded to the front of the van, while I slowed down. Beth and Paula were twisting John's head in the proper direction saying, "John! John! look at the elephant! Right there. Just like Horton in your book." "Say, John," I said, "Maybe that's Horton. Maybe he's the one who sat on the egg." "Yeah, Horton," said John. "Why's he all red colored." Stephen asked. "Well, he dusts his back with the red soil for some reason. Maybe he just likes to roll in the dirt." I said. That satisfied everyone. "He just likes to roll in the dirt." It's surprising how little you need to explain things to young children. If they ask a question that you don't know, you can just say "Because" and that will satisfy them most of the time.

The elephant didn't seem to be in a hurry. He was just ambling down the middle of the road. As Stephen had observed, his back was a dusty-looking red color. We took pictures, but he didn't turn around. All we could see was a big hulk of red elephant backsides with a little tail. I am glad he didn't turn around. There was no place for me to go. The road is only two narrow lanes with a two or three foot bank on each side. We didn't follow too close. I didn't want to disturb him, after all—he had the right of way. The elephant finally decided to go off through the grass and left the road to us.

Elephants not only have the right of way for cars, they have the right of way for trains as well. The following article is from the *East African Standard:*

LINE BLOCKED AFTER ELEPHANT DERAILMENT

The railway line which was damaged when a goods train was derailed after hitting a herd of elephants as they crossed the line between Mkomba and Mikumi stations on Wednesday will not be repaired for two days a spokesman for the East African Railways and Harbors said.

Four elephants and a calf walked onto the line at the time of the collision. The driver of the train was the only crew member to escape without injury.

Off to the right of the road, we saw Lake Nakuru. We were driving along an escarpment which gave us a good view of the lake and surrounding valley. It looked as though it had a wide sand beach around the entire shoreline. As we got closer to the lake, we realized it wasn't a sandy beach we had been looking at; but, rather a broad band of flamingos. This swath of thousands of flamingos must have been 200 to 300 feet wide. There were so many of these birds—thousands and thousands of them. They were all feeding in the ankle-deep water along the shoreline. It was lunch time, and we sat down on one of the picnic tables and ate the sandwiches we had packed for the trip. There was no problem with the kids trying to feed the birds. There is a deep muck around the shoreline preventing anyone from approaching the flamingos, which stand in the water beyond the muck. It looked much nicer from the road than up close.

It was about 2 p.m. when we pulled into the compound of the African Inland Mission on the outskirts of Nairobi. The AIM people had done the same thing as the Tororo Girls School faculty. We had both created an American neighborhood in the middle of Africa. I think that every culture does that. Many large cities in the States have a Chinatown section. In San Francisco's Chinatown, McDonald's restaurant has a menu written in Chinese on the wall behind the counter. Here in Kenya, we were standing in the middle of the African Inland Mission compound, hearing English spoken in American accents, seeing American young people playing basketball, and even smelling American-type food cooking in the kitchens. Oh, did that seem good. We were home.

I admire the missionary doctors who work in the African Inland Mission in Kenya. They could be living the "good life" back in the States. Why do they choose to live here? I wonder if there isn't a little bit of "adventurer" in every missionary. But, who am I to judge that. It was the adventure and opportunity to travel that had brought me to TGS.

There was a small infirmary that served as a hospital at AIM. We inquired and were directed to the office in the front part of the infirmary. The woman at the desk greeted us, and I told her my story. We were from Tororo, Uganda, and had been told that we might find American doctors at AIM. We were directed to the house of one of the doctors on the compound. We left the car where it was parked, walked over to the house, knocked at the kitchen screen door, and were greeted with a "Come on in." It was like visiting friends. The doctor was reading something that looked more like work than fun. His wife was busy with kitchen duties and two small children who were playing on the kitchen floor.

I introduced myself and family, and we met Jim and Cheryl Robinson—nice people. After telling our Tororo story and stateside experience and training, we got down to the reason for our visit. "Well, you see, Jim, we've all been feeling sick. We've lost appetite, can't sleep well, and have stomach cramps. I thought it might be a cold or flu coming on, but I'm not sure and want to have a professional opinion."

"We'll have to take blood tests, X-rays, and get a stool sample. We don't have the sophisticated equipment that you're used to in New York, so it will take a couple of days before we can make a diagnosis. Why don't we get started right now. I'll walk you over to the infirmary, and we can take a blood sample and do some X-rays today. I'll get some containers for your stool sample. We should have the results back in a couple of days. You can stay with us here. We have a guesthouse that we use for missionaries who come in from the bush." Jim said.

As we walked over to the infirmary, the compound elementary school was letting out. There were not a lot of children—probably less than 20. Paula, Beth, and Stephen seemed shy as the missionary kids tagged along with us on our walk to the infirmary. "What's your name?" These MKS (missionary kids) were asking our children. Paula, Beth, and Stephen, muttered their names in quiet voices. John said, "I'm John, and I'm three and a half, and we saw an elephant today, and a giraffe, and a lot of ah, ah, Dad what were those birds?" "Flamingos," John, I replied. "Yea, those," said John. John was having trouble saying "flamingos."

John was not so happy in the infirmary when he saw the syringes being prepared for us. "No one likes shots, son," Jim said, "but after the blood work, we'll go out and see the parrot. It can talk. Did you ever hear a bird talk?" Jim went on with this conversation while he rubbed a spot on John's arm and inserted the syringe. Paula was worse than John, her face was squeezed up and she was squealing "Ahh, Ahh, Ooo, Ooo." This didn't help Beth who was starting to cry. Stephen was not crying, but he looked nervous. The X-rays were painless, and we were finally done with the hard part. Now all we had to do was return our little plastic stool sample containers the next morning.

We left the infirmary, got our luggage out of the car, and transferred it to the guesthouse. It was a small cottage with a kitchen, bath, living room, and three bedrooms—very clean, very American, and very "missionary" with the occasional framed Bible text on the walls. There were also some original oils of African wild life with the signature "Jim Robinson." As it turned out, Jim is a very good artist. His paintings are professional quality.

As we were exploring our quarters, Cheryl knocked on the guesthouse door. "Jim and I would like to have you over tonight for dinner. You can't say "No. " because it's doctor's orders, and that settles it. We'll be eating at six. You can relax, freshen up, and then come over about quarter of six.

We had dinner that night with Jim and Cheryl and their three children—all girls. Stephen didn't like that very much, but our girls loved it. That evening we met another missionary couple, Mark and Sarah Adams. Mark and Sarah were as friendly as Jim and Cheryl. That evening Mark said, "Tomorrow we're going hunting down in the Rift Valley. Why don't you come with us? Every few months, we get a permit from the Kenyan Government to hunt for meat. They give us a specific parcel of land for 24 hours. During that time, a tract of several square miles will be exclusively ours to hunt on. No one else can use it during that time period. We're allowed to have guns here, but they must be stored at the police station when we're not hunting. There's a limit on the kind of animals we take. We also have to pay a certain rate for each species. Why don't you, your wife, and the kids come along. We'll leave about ten tomorrow morning, drive down in the Rift, and set up the tents. Then we'll spend the night in our tents and come back the next morning."

I couldn't believe my ears. Hunting in Africa! "Wow, kids, want to go hunting tomorrow?" Of course, everyone wanted to go. The rest of the evening was spent talking about the next day's adventure. That night we all went to bed thinking of hunting in Africa. I was so happy that I had decided to find American doctors and the African Inland Mission.

The first thing I noticed about Kenya was that it's colder in the mornings than Tororo. It felt like a spring morning with a temperature of about 50 to 60 degrees. I noticed that Africans walking along the road were wearing woolen sweaters. We had also seen flocks of sheep.

The hunting parcel that Mark had been assigned was about a half-hour's drive from the AIM compound. AIM is located on the east escarpment; the hunting parcel is just down the escarpment in the valley below. There aren't many roads in the Rift Valley, but the driving isn't difficult. One simply drives down the road to the proper section assigned and turns off into the grassland. It's just a big, level field with occasional trees. Mark located our assigned parcel, we drove across the field, and camped under some tall trees. I'm not sure what kind of trees these were, but they looked like the trees we call buttonwood in New York. After we stopped, we all got out and put up the tents. I saw the remains of a campfire with a circle of stones and some ashes. It was like camping on a lawn with shade trees. The cars were parked in a circle around the lawn area. The tents were set up on the lawn, a fire was started with some of the fallen branches we found around the trees, and we were ready to hunt.

Mark had decided what was needed to replenish their freezers with meat. He wanted one kongoni and one warthog. The kongoni is a deer-like animal but much larger. The warthog is a pig. The warthog is smaller than the pigs I had seen in the States—approximately a half to a third the size.

The first part of hunting is scouting the area to find where the particular type of animal is that you want. Mark had the rifle, so he was doing the hunting, and I had a van that would accommodate the hunting party. I drove, and Jim helped spotting.

Hunting in Africa isn't like hunting in New York. When I go deer hunting in New York, I get up early in the morning, drive to a State Forest Land, park the car, tramp though the woods for an hour or so, and hope something walks past that I get a shot at. There have been entire days when I haven't seen a deer. It was a family joke. "There goes Dad on his winter picnic." I would stand out in the cold woods, (It's best to hunt deer when there's snow on the ground.) drink my coffee, eat my sandwich, and then go home. I finally gave up on that. I'm just not a hunter. In Africa hunting is like going to the supermarket. You just make your selection and shoot.

We drove through the grass—six to eight inches tall—about a mile or two from the campsite. Herds of various species of animals came into view. We saw zebra, waterbuck, antelope, gazelle, warthog, and some ostrich. We came upon a herd of kongoni. That's what Mark wanted. There must have been a few hundred kongoni in the herd. They were all just grazing in the field. The kongoni didn't seem alarmed that we were driving up in the van. It seemed like driving across a field to a herd of cows. We stopped the van and started looking for the exact kongoni that Mark wanted to shoot.

When Mark made his selection, he asked me to let him out and drive slowly around the perimeter of the herd. As I started driving, Mark opened the door and stepped out of the van. I drove slowly around the herd—this was about a mile—and circled back to Mark. When we got to Mark he had already shot his kongoni. Mark gutted the kongoni, which we draped over the roof of the van and returned to camp. The entire process took less than an hour. When we arrived back at camp, the women had water boiling and were ready to start preparing our kongoni dinner. After a portion of the kongoni was selected for the evening meal, the carcass was hung from a tree. Mark had a long, sturdy rope which he tied around the kongoni's feet and threw over a high branch. The kongoni was then hoisted about 15 feet off the ground. It was lifted high enough so that lions couldn't reach it. "Lions?" I asked. "Lions, do we have lions here?" "Of course there are lions, and they will smell the kill. That is why I gutted the kongoni out of camp." Mark explained.

The rest of the day was spent driving around the grassland looking at animals, chasing ostrich with the car, and hunting warthogs. Warthog hunting is more challenging than kongoni hunting. These little pigs scoot through the grass with their tails sticking up in the air. We dropped Mark off and tried to herd the warthogs to him, but without success. We didn't get a warthog that day. While we were driving through the grassland, we came across the remains of a zebra. The carcass was covered with vultures who were fighting among themselves for the meat. They wouldn't move for the van, and at one point, I drove the van right over the zebra bones. The vultures stayed on the bones and would not budge out of the way. I could hear the van hitting the vultures—thump, thump, thump—as my VW passed over. The zebra had been stripped of its hide and the rest left for the vultures. "That's your big game hunter," Mark said.

That evening we sat around the campfire listening to tales of other hunts, and enjoying roast kongoni. Just about the time we were thinking of going to bed, I heard a "GGGRUNT!" "GGGRUNT!" "GGGRUNT!" Turning to Mark I said, "What's that!" "Lions, just lions." Mark replied. "They smell the meat and come around the campsite at night. Don't worry, we have the kongoni hoisted out of their reach." "But," I said "We're in the tents!" "Oh, they won't bother us." Nevertheless, I put the sleeping children on the seats inside the van and closed the doors. Then I took the campfire axe, crawled into the tent, and waited for the lions to attack.

The next morning I heard Mark outside the tent saying, "Where's the axe? Has anybody seen the axe? I need to chop some firewood." I stuck my head out the tent flap and said, "Here's the axe, Mark." Mark cocked his head and said, "What are you doing with the axe in your tent?" "Well," I replied, "I wanted some protection against the lions, and you've got the gun." Mark laughed. "Right, I can just picture you flaying around in the dark with an axe."

Masai warrior who walked into our camp in the Rift Valley seeking water.

We were taking down the tents and loading the cars to return to AIM when I looked over by the trees and saw John looking up at a Masai warrior with a spear. I don't know where he came from or how he could have walked into camp without anyone seeing him. We were in the middle of a grassland that was hundreds of miles long and at least 30 miles wide. But, there he was. He was a young man, I would guess in his middle twenties, dressed in the traditional red colored, knee-length costume that is tied over one shoulder. In his hand he carried a 5-foot long spear. As I said, we didn't see him approaching at all. He just seemed to appear. It was a strange sight to see this tribal warrior among a group of western-dressed white men, women, and children. I walked over to rescue John. The Masai didn't seem hostile, and John wasn't afraid of him. Wow! A tribesman with a spear. John was not saying anything, which was unusual, because John was always talking, talking, talking. John and the Masai were just silently looking at each other. "Hey, Mark," I called out. "Here's a Masai." I had seen these people in the *National Geographic* and knew that they lived in the Rift Valley; but, somehow, it had never occurred to me that I might actually meet one. "See what he wants." Mark replied. Mark didn't seem upset. So, I thought this must be normal. I used what little Swahili I knew and said "Jambo" (Hello) to which he replied, "Jambo." So, he spoke Swahili. I went on with the rest of the greeting, "Habari." (this is actually the word "news" but is a short cut version of "How are you doing?") The Masai said, "Maji." (water). "Hey, Mark," I called out. "He wants water." Cheryl took an empty mayonnaise jar from the kitchen box, unscrewed the top, filled it with water, screwed the top back on, and called to John. "John, give this water to the man." John took the jar from Cheryl and carried it over to the

Masai. This must have been a strange sight to John. I wonder what he was thinking? He was very, very quiet. The Masai took the mayonnaise jar from John and just looked at it. He held it up to the sun, shook it, turned it over in his hand, and placed it on the ground. "Hey, Mark, this guy won't drink it." I called out. "He probably doesn't know how to get the top off. Remove the top for him," Mark called back. All the time this was going on, everyone else was busy packing the cars. I picked the jar up from the ground, held it up before the Masai's face, and unscrewed the top. Then I tipped the jar and let a small bit of the water pour out in my hand. He said, "Ennh!" and took the proffered mayonnaise jar of water. He drank the water—all of it, and then he sat down with his back against the tree trying to put the lid back on. He was turning the lid in the wrong direction—unscrewing it, and it wouldn't go back on. All the while we packed the cars he sat underneath the tree turning the lid backward. As we left, I could see him in my rear view mirror still trying to replace the lid. I wonder if he ever did? Somewhere in the Rift Valley there is a Miracle Whip jar and a blue top. I wonder if the top is on the jar? I'll never know.

When we returned to the AIM compound, I asked Mark about the Masai visitor we had. "You know, Mark, I've been told that Masai warriors cover their spear edges with a cow hide strip that protects the sharp edge from getting dull. I'm also told that these spears are greased with cow fat when they're going to be used. That Masai's spear didn't have the protective strip on it, and it was coated with grease. How come? He seemed friendly enough to me." "Well," Mark replied, "To be a warrior a young man must kill a lion by himself. He then brings back evidence of the kill to the tribe. Until he does this, he's not allowed to have a bride or be considered a man. I would guess that this Masai was hunting lion, and had his spear ready for a lion kill. He must have walked a long distance. He was thirsty, and he was the only Masai we saw during our trip back. He was out alone, trying to kill a lion."

The rest of the African people I met were trying to be Europeans. They dressed like Europeans, learned English, wore shoes—even if these were made from car tires, rode bicycles, sent their children to European schools, and even tried to make their skin light. Ambi cream does that for them. This is a big seller in Uganda. Ambi cream is rubbed on the skin and it bleaches the skin a pink-white color. It wasn't uncommon to see Africans in town with pink-white faces, necks, arms, and black legs.

This Masai seemed to be proud of who he was and what he looked like. He could be called a "noble" African. Not trying to be African. something he wasn't. The Masai have turned their backs on European culture. They consider it inferior to their own. Mark told me the story of one Masai that an AIM missionary met while hunting. The missionary came across a Masai who could speak English. That was so unusual that he asked, "How do you know English?" To which the Masai replied, "I attended a mission school and have an honor's degree from Bonn University in Germany." "Then what are you doing dressed like this? Have you forgotten what you learned in mission school?" Pointing to the missionary's watch, the Masai replied, "Your God is on your wrist. You get up in the morning when your God tells you, you eat when your God tells you, and you go to sleep at night when your God tells you. I get up, eat, and go to sleep when I wish. The Masai culture is superior to your culture. Masai villages do not have the crime that western cultures have. The

Masai people are content and happy, your people aren't. Why should I give up what I have for your culture?"

Technology will be the death of the Masai one day. These proud people will either have to change or be destroyed. A spear is no match for a rifle, and the medicine man can't compete with science and modern technology. I don't know whether I feel sad about this or not. I just feel privileged to have met this Masai and to have seen his tribal nobility. We returned to the AIM compound, and went to the guest house where we showered and changed our clothes. Somehow we had all grown a little from our day in the Rift Valley.

The test results showed that we had a parasite infestation. "You all have roundworms." the doctor said. "If you have a houseboy preparing your food, I would guess that it's due to fecal contamination. If your cook doesn't wash his hands prior to food preparation, you're going to have a recurrence of the problem. I suggest that you give him this brush to use with soap and water on his hands after every bowel movement. You must impress upon him that he do this. I've given you a prescription for a tablet to be taken every day for ten days. I'm also giving you a prescription for any future episodes you may have. It can be purchased in any pharmacy in East Africa. This is not uncommon, and these tablets are readily available."

"What did the doctor say," Stephen asked. I smiled and said, "He thinks we're full of worms." "Yeah," John said, "Full of worms."

15

Nairobi is a half-hour's drive from African Inland Mission. As we approached the city, we passed a group of African women making and selling baskets at the side of the road. The mornings are colder in Nairobi than in Tororo. These basket makers wore woolen sweaters over their dresses as they sat on the ground weaving the baskets. It reminded me of the Native American women that I have often seen at a rest stop just south of Flagstaff, Arizona, selling jewelry. However, none of these Kenyan vendors spoke English; so we fumbled along in our poor Swahili bargaining prices with them. I felt like an old-timer after just six months in East Africa. These basket makers are far enough away from the city of Nairobi to exclude tourists, so the prices are lower than those found in either Kampala or Nairobi. The selection of baskets ranged from laundry-size to drinking-glass coasters. These baskets are made of tan-colored wicker with decorative bands of green, red, yellow, and black. In the States these baskets and mats would have been hung on the wall as "art." In Kenya and Uganda they were used for what they are—laundry baskets and drinking glass coasters.

Nairobi didn't look African. It looked like a European city. There are as many white people on the streets of Nairobi as there are blacks. As we walked along the street past the Nairobi Hilton, I could identify French, German,

Basket makers along the road.

Italian, and Japanese languages as well as English spoken with British, American, and Canadian accents. There are several "quaint shops" featuring etched glassware, African pottery, exotic leather goods, safari clothing, and carved wooden items—all very nice, and all very expensive. Nairobi is a place for the wealthy tourist.

The Nairobi Hilton is as modern as any of the Hilton hotels in the States, but more expensive. Americans can fly into Nairobi on an American Airlines plane, travel from the airport on an American Airlines shuttle bus, get off at the American Hilton Hotel, take the Otis elevator to the 15th floor, open the door to their "luxury" room, and turn on the color TV. "Hey, honey, call room service and have some hot dogs, French fries and a six-pack of

Budweiser sent up. It's almost time for the Yankee's game. Isn't it great to be in Africa?"

The Nairobi Hilton is not our Africa. We *live* here, and we've got the worms to prove it, just ask John. "Isn't that right, John?" "Yeah, we're full of worms."

The Gatchell's told us about the Fair View—choice of the expatriate crowd. The Fair View is a hotel in a residential section of Nairobi. It's a ten-minute drive from downtown Nairobi. The street is lined with large, old stone houses and beautifully landscaped grounds. As we approached the Fair View, we passed the embassies of several nations. These have broad stone driveways with uniformed guards at the gates. The absence of safari-suited tourists made us feel like we were in a place where people lived, not a movie set. The only people in these tan safari jackets, and Australian-type cowboy hats are tourists. They look like actors in an old African movie. As close as people living in Africa come to looking like that are the British with tan shorts and knee socks.

The Fair View hotel looks like an embassy compound with its manicured lawns, trees, and flower beds. It's just the spot for families with small children. The main part of the hotel is quartered in a large, old castle-type building which has some single rooms, a pub, a "telly" room, and a dining hall. The larger family-sized rooms are in a separate building of newer construction located behind the main building. This newer building is like many of the motel chains found in the States. Clean and comfortable with no frills. The Fair View caters to families with small children. There is an evening "children's dinner" served in a cafeteria-style atmosphere. The menu items are suited to a child's taste, but decidedly British with the traditional spaghetti, fish and chips, and cheese sandwiches we had found in other areas of East Africa. The children eat earlier than the adults. Mothers supervise the children during this children's meal, while the men retreat to the pub in the next room. The children's dinner is a noisy time with babies crying, plates and silverware dropping, and young children laughing and yelling to be heard. It is much the same as a grade-school lunchtime in the States. The one visible distinction is the presence of African female house servants caring for children. The Fair View has African women on staff who will babysit the children of patrons during this children's meal. A husband and wife can hire a resident babysitter to supervise their children's dining and then stay in the hotel room for the evening if the parents want a "night on the town."

We checked into the Fair View, found our room, unpacked our luggage, and went out to look about the grounds. The kids, of course, were most interested in the playground area. There are swings, slides, ropes, ladders to climb, and what John loved best—a big, pink pig on a heavy spring. He would climb on this pig, sit in the saddle on its back, grab the handles sprouting from the pig's ears, and rock back and forth while I gave him the old Arkansas cheer—"Go you hog! Go!" He loved it. There were plenty of empty swings and not many children on the slides, so Stephen, Paula, and Beth, were able to work off some energy. Enough, I hoped, so that they would be ready for bed soon after the children's meal. Their mother and I had tickets to theater in Nairobi for that evening.

After an hour or so on the playground equipment, and some running around on the grass, the kids were getting hungry. British children do not play baseball or basketball. They were playing soccer on the lawn. We didn't know anything about soccer, so the kids just chased each other. "Dad," Paula and Beth said, "We're hungry." Stephen said he was hungry also. It was time for the children's meal, so we took the kids into the dining room and sat down. There were long rows of tables and along one wall there were a number of high chairs. The children sat down and picked up a menu. The selections were typically British. There was canned spaghetti, fish and chips, steak and kidney pie, shepherd's pie, cheese and crackers, and cereal. The dessert choices were cake, cookies, ice cream, and pudding. There were also bowls of fruit on the table.

Our kids had grown fond of shepherd's pie, which is ground beef and gravy over mashed potatoes. This was followed by ice cream. Ice cream was a big treat for the children in Africa. It is impossible to find ice cream in Tororo.

After the children's meal, we all went into the "telly" room. This was the only TV set we had seen in six months. Nairobi has just one television channel. Having only one channel eliminates arguments over what to watch. The programming on African TV is not very good. We watched an old rerun of *I Dream of Jeannie.* Had we been in the States, none of us would have been interested in this program. However, we were doing something "American" in Africa. Just like the tourists at the Hilton, only our choices both at the table and in the "telly" room were much more limited. After Jeannie was put back in her bottle, the kids were starting to get tired and cranky. It was time to get back to the room, and put the kids in bed.

The children were all sleeping when the African babysitter arrived. Joyce and I changed our clothes and drove into Nairobi for the theater.

The brightly-lit streets in the center of the city were quieter than they had been during the day. Most of the "quaint shops" were closed. However, the Hilton was still busy with tourists arriving and departing on airport shuttle busses, and the restaurants and swanky tourist bars were busy.

Theater in Nairobi is not a tourist attraction. The acting was performed by a local acting group who have full-time jobs and participate in these plays for something to do in their leisure time. The performances are held in a school auditorium-type building, somewhat like an "off-Broadway" setting. That evening the play was *Mame,* which had been around for a while. The acting wasn't that good; but, as I said, it was something for the actors and the patrons to do in Africa.

"Something to do" in Africa. For the tourist there is always something to do. The game parks, "quaint shops," Treetops, Mount Kilimanjaro, the Nile, Mombasa, the Indian Ocean—the elephants, the giraffe, the lions! However, the tourist is in Africa for two or three weeks. What do Europeans—and I use that term in its broadest sense to include Americans—do if they live and work in Africa? Being the member of a local acting group would be "fun," especially when compared to chess, BBC shortwave, tennis, or swimming. There were days in Tororo when George Andrezejewski and I played chess for the entire day—30 or more games of chess! Now, that's entertainment!

The Fair View's room price included breakfast—juice, coffee, cereal, eggs, and bacon—"burn" the bacon. If bacon is crispy, the British call it "burned." We were up early, and ready for a day's sightseeing in Nairobi. While we were eating our burned bacon and taking our worm pill, I said, "How would you kids like to go to a game park?"

Actually, we were taking two pills that morning. We took our prophylactic malaria pill every morning. There were several kinds of anti-malaria medicine. East Africa is an area where one must have protection from malaria. We chose a little white pill that was so bitter it had to be held between the teeth and washed down with liquid. If the pill touched your tongue, it was very bad tasting. It was a simple process—hold the pill between the front teeth, put the glass to your lips, and release the pill with the first swallow. It was hard to teach the children this trick. There's a clear, tasteless, colorless liquid that can be used for children. It looks like water and is easier for the children to use, but we chose the bitter pill. One American missionary family in East Africa used the clear, liquid type of anti-malarial medicine. They had two small children. One child died after drinking an entire bottle of this medicine. Shortly after, their second child died in the same way. We felt that this clear, tasteless medicine was poison just waiting for its next small victim. The kids would never have been able to ingest the little, bitter pills that we had on the breakfast table.

After breakfast we drove into Nairobi in search of film, binoculars, and a good camera. A camera and binoculars are the staples of a tourist's diet in East Africa. The Hilton hotel is the center of the tourist mecca of Nairobi. We parked the VW and started looking in the "quaint shops" for a camera. As we walked down the street, I saw a small truck with a platform where the truck "box" is usually located. On this "flatbed" was a large tripod with a camera and telephoto lens that was four or five feet long. On the side of the truck was the seal of the National Geographic Society. I stopped and talked with an American who was sitting in the truck. "Wow!" I said, "That's a monster camera. I'll bet you could take pictures of the Empire State Building from here with a telephoto lens that size." The man smiled and said, "Not quite, but we can get a good shot of Trafalgar Square in London." We talked about cameras, lenses, film, and what equipment I would need to get some good pictures while living in East Africa. "Well," the man said. "This is one of the best places I can think of to purchase photographic equipment. The selection is large, and the prices are much lower than the States. Try that shop," he said, pointing across the street. We went in the small store and came out with a 35 mm camera, a telephoto lens, and a pair of binoculars. We were ready for our first game park!

In addition to the game park, there was one other thing we wanted to do in Nairobi. We had been told about Bazaar Street by several people both at TGS and at The Fair View. "If you're in Nairobi, you've got to see Bazaar Street." So, off we went from the "quaint shops" area of Nairobi in search of Bazaar Street. It's not hard to find this street. All you have to do is follow your nose" so to speak. Bazaar Street is the area of Nairobi where the Indian—"Asian"—shops are located. The entire street is nestled in the middle of the most delicious smelling aroma of curry. We are partial to "spicy" food, and just walking down Bazaar Street at any time of the day or night is a delight to the senses.

The street is lined on both sides with open-air shops that sell spices, wood carvings of the highest-quality workmanship, African artifacts, and colorful clothing. The clothing shops are interesting. There are bolts of cloth hanging on the walls of these shops. One selects the particular cloth wanted, the style of shirt or dress desired, and is measured by the clerk. Stephen, John, and I choose shirts. Joyce, Paula, and Beth chose dresses. We all chose a popular African print that we had seen both in Uganda and Kenya. This particular print is available only in East Africa. Having a shirt or dress made from this particular cotton madras is the "I've been there."

badge of the traveler. It's like belonging to a "secret club." "Oh, I see you've been in East Africa. I have one also." That kind of thing. We chose the cloth and pattern, were measured, and were told to come back in a couple of hours.

For the next two hours we walked up and down Bazaar Street treasure hunting. There were no safari suits on Bazaar Street: so, we knew we were in the right place for bargains. As I mentioned, the street had open-air shops on both sides. When the shops open in the morning, the gates are unlocked and opened exposing three inner walls with long tables in the middle displaying the wares. Most of the people in the shops and on the street are Asian. The men are dressed in long, white cotton robes with a turban and sandals. The veiled women wear brightly-colored saris with a decorative red dot in the middle of their forehead and a jewel in their nose.

There are shops that sell fresh fruits and vegetables. One Indian dish I particularly like is called "chaioda." This is a snack food made of fried rice, lentils, and nuts which is roasted and seasoned with curry. I had one of the Asian students at Tororo Girls School make some of this for us. She also gave us the recipe.

In addition to the clothing and foods, there are shops selling carvings. Of all the wood carvings I have seen in Africa, none compare in quality with those I saw on Bazaar Street. In addition to the traditional African animal and people figures, there were "Indian-style" carvings, both figures and tables. We purchased a three-legged table of Indian design. Each leg is the figure of an elephant head and trunk. The round top is inlaid with small ivory figures. It's a beautiful piece.

After we had walked up and down Bazaar Street, we returned to the shop where our shirts and dresses were

Baboons jump on cars waiting for treats. Keep your windows closed!

being made. In front of the shop, some tailors were sewing our clothing together with treadle sewing machines. These items were just about finished, and we watched the final stitches. When they were finished, we returned to the Fair View where we had lunch, and relaxed while John took his nap prior to the Game Park trip we had planned for the afternoon.

    Nairobi National Park is a good place for one to start building a photo album of animals. It's a 20-minute drive from downtown Nairobi and is more of an open-air zoo than a game park. You pay the entrance fee and drive through the park taking pictures of the animals that are roaming about freely. This area does not have numbers, but a large variety of non-predator wildlife. There are many varieties of deerlike animals, from the small dik dik, to the large water buffalo. There is also a variety of birds and reptiles. However, don't get out of your car. You can purchase biscuits to feed animals from the car windows. Don't roll the windows down too far. We saw a baboon reach into a car and rip an expensive camera out of the hands of one man that day. The man had his window all the way down and was trying to take a picture of a baboon, when ZAP! There went the camera bounding across the field in the hands of the baboon. I wonder how many cameras, binoculars, and purses that baboon has collected. He seemed to know just what he was doing.

We had a full day in Nairobi and had been to our first game park. I don't think that we ever got tired of seeing animals. I thought back to the day in Alfred when I had asked the kids, "Hey, kids, How would you like to go to Africa and see the animals—the elephants, the lions, the giraffe?" Well, here we were doing just that.

Late that afternoon we drove back to the Fair View. We took some great pictures and sent some postcards home. Now that the day's activity was over, we were homesick again. Whenever things slowed down for us, our thoughts went back to the States and family. "I wonder how Vicky is?" Stephen asked. "I wish Grampa and Gramma were here." Beth said.

We started back to Tororo the next morning. On our way out of Nairobi we stopped and purchased some baskets, looked at the flamingos at Lake Navasha, and ate lunch at "The Bell." Other than the sign saying ELEPHANTS HAVE THE RIGHT OF WAY, the only additional sign I remember on that road was one that says EAT WELL AT THE BELL. The Bell is a small diner in Nakuru. As we approached the Uganda/Kenya border, the air became warmer, and the grasslands gave way to banana trees.

There were more people walking along the road. We stopped at the border, showed our passports, and drove back to our house at TGS.

It was good to see the Gatchells and Andrezejewskis again. The children were full of stories of the trip and eager to play with their friends again. So, here we were back. Bill and I were talking about USAID, U Mass, Doubleday, Roop, and Williams; while the kids played centipede hockey on the porch.

"Bill," I said, "when we were at the Fair View I met an old British expatriate who told me how the Africans in Kenya catch elephants. First they dig a big pit in the ground. Then they line the edge of the pit with peas. When this is done, they hide in the bushes. When an elephant passes by and stops to take a pea, they all rush out and push him in the pit." "Very funny," said Gatchell.

16

The Christmas vacation was drawing to a close, and the students would be returning soon for the next semester at Tororo Girls School. I had been busy preparing for their return. The typewriters were all working, the books were stacked in the front of the room waiting to be passed out, and course outlines were prepared for my second semester at TGS.

In the main building of TGS there is a faculty mailroom where in addition to mailboxes, there is a bulletin board which contains items of interest to all faculty members. As I was leaving the mailroom one day, I saw the following letter from the mother of one of our students, Gaudensia Ongura. It read:

P.O. Box 3525
Kumki, Teso

Dear Miss Phyllis,

Thank you very much for yours which I got dated 12th sympathizing with me and my family. About my daughter's death, I blame the doctors only because, they took her to the hospital where mad people are treated, yet she was not mad at all. It was too much of malaria which went and disturbed her brain and made her like a mad person. So, what they did was to treat her like a mad person in Butabika Hospital. When they saw that she was seriously sick, then they took her to Mulago Hospital where she died after two days. She was brought home on the 8th and buried on the same day. So, there is nothing to worry too much about anymore, since we can do nothing but mourning only. Her body is hidden safely.

I humbly and kindly ask you to take the remaining daughter I have next year for S.II please. I shall try as hard as I can to pay her school fees. If she also dies before me than I bury her also, since I can do nothing.

Thank you for the memorial service you held on the 14th. I hope God will hear our prayers. Pass my greetings to all her schoolmates and classmates and tell them that she wished with all her heart to say goodbye to them if they were near. And to Father Van Gestel whom she knew very well plus the staff members.

All we can do about this matter is to pray for her soul and to rest in peace.

I remain sincerely
Matiasi Ongura

This student had malaria, but the African medical officers administering aid decided she was insane and put her in a mental hospital. In this mental hospital she would have simply been confined with insane people. A proper diagnosis should have started with a thermometer. This would have shown an elevated temperature, and treatment could have gone on from that point. Life in Africa is so very fragile. When leaving each other, this girl's tribal custom was not to say "goodbye," but rather "Mami Twani," which means "Don't die."

The medical facilities in Uganda are very poor. The American Embassy's Health and Medical Information Sheet hints at this. This information sheet starts out with a disclaimer:

> The following information is designed to assist American employees of State, USIS, USAID, and PC in obtaining

medical aid for themselves and their families. The inclusion of the names of individuals and institutions in this information sheet is not meant to imply recommendation of any.

The *Ugandan Argus* carried the following story while we were in Tororo.

KEROSENE TRANSFUSION IN ERROR

The findings of an inquest into the death of a woman patient. Mrs. Selina Mugoga Lunani at Kakamega General Hospital last July from kerosene poisoning—mistakenly transfused into her body in place of fruit salt—was brought before the Kakamega resident magistrate's court yesterday.

The magistrate, Mr. Amin, ruled that there was no doubt that Mrs. Lunani died of shock, due to multiple embolism of kerosene poisoning. He added that this was, however, not due to negligence on the part of any member of the hospital staff.

The court was told that a hospital assistant had discovered the transfusion to be of paraffin when the patient's condition became worse. On removing the transfusion needle, he felt the tip and found it "oily."

On a closer examination, he discovered that the content in bottle from which the solution came was actually paraffin.

He immediately called in senior medical officers who took up the matter for investigation.

The court was also told that the officer on duty had been actually administering treatment as prescribed by the medical officer. He had collected a bottle bearing a saline label, but the solution inside was not saline but kerosene mistakenly placed in the same cupboard with other saline bottles.

I am glad to read, "This was, however, not due to negligence on the part of any member of the hospital staff." It just happened. I can't imagine a patient being given a transfusion of kerosene instead of fruit salt in the States. The doctors, nurses, and hospital would "have a lot of 'splainin' " to do.

There is a hospital in Tororo, and I knew the Korean doctor who was a surgeon there. I asked Dr. Kim if I could take some pictures of Tororo Hospital to show our family and friends in the States. He thought that was a great idea and set a time when I could come to the hospital. He said I could take all the pictures I wanted.

Tororo Hospital consists of four, single-story buildings of wooden construction. One building is the out-patient clinic, there are two wards—one surgical and one maternity. The fourth building houses a pharmacy and operating room. These buildings are small. The maternity and surgical wards have 20 beds each, and the other two buildings are the roughly the same size.

I arrived at the hospital at approximately 10 a.m. The out-patient clinic had a crowd of about 80 people who were standing and sitting on the ground outside the door waiting to be seen by the "medical officer." Everyone must wait his turn, no matter what the problem is. This can a predicament if one has been bitten by a poisonous snake. The patient could die waiting in line to see the medical officer. After being seen by the medical officer, I am not sure just what happens. There were no Europeans or Asians in this line. This is the very last place I would go if I needed medical treatment of any kind. The medical officers at Tororo Hospital are allowed to take a patient's temperature by axilla (armpit) method only. That is, of course, if a thermometer is available.

The maternity ward consists of twenty beds—ten beds on each side of the room. These metal cots have two upright, iron poles at the foot of the bed which support a basket for the baby. When I arrived, the patients were standing on the lawn outside the building holding their babies because the floors were being mopped. Most African women give birth at home. In fact, the *Uganda Argus* carried the story of a bride who gave birth at her wedding:

THE UNEXPECTED GUEST

A bride who was married near Masaka Town gave birth to a child at the wedding party. The news was kept secret at the time of entertaining guests.

When an African woman is in labor, she isn't going to be able to walk miles to the hospital from her village. The women in this maternity ward were probably wives of African men who worked in Tororo and, therefore, not living in their home village. The only other beds in this hospital were in the surgical ward. The last building I took pictures of contained a pharmacy and the operating room. I remember seeing 15 or 20 gallon-size bottles of liquid in the pharmacy. I didn't know what these bottles contained. The African tending this room didn't speak English and my Swahili vocabulary did not accommodate medical/technical conversations.

As I was about to leave the Pharmacy, Dr. Kim came in and said, "This is a very good day for you to be here. I am about to repair a hernia. You must come in and take pictures of the operation." I wasn't sure I wanted to do that; but, after all, I was only allowed to take pictures of the hospital because of Dr. Kim's kindness and permission. So, off we went to the operating room. I thought I would have to put on a special gown, have a special mask, wash my hands, or do something. That wasn't the case. I simply walked into a room where a naked African man was lying on a table under a big light. Dr. Kim wore rubber gloves, a gown, and a face mask. He had already given the man some kind of anesthetic, so the operation was about to begin.

Dr. Kim was delighted to have me watch him operate. He was joking with me as he started. "We have to keep the windows open or we would roast in here. However, it isn't possible to get screens for the windows in East Africa; so I have to keep picking flies out of the incision. They dive down into the incision like Kamikaze pilots." Ha, Ha, Ha, he laughed. With this, he drew his scalpel across the man's abdomen exposing a layer of yellow fat tissue; then he sliced down through this yellow layer into the red muscle which he parted into the abdominal cavity. Now he was getting into it. "These people have poor muscle tissue because of lack of protein in their diet. The muscle just pulls apart like cooked meat. I do a lot of hernia repair here. With the least little abdominal stress the muscle tissue tears. I must use heavy suture material with wide stitches, or the suture material just pulls through the muscle." I was starting to feel light-headed. I had a prickly sensation across my forehead, and I knew that I was going to faint if I kept watching this operation. I looked just above Dr. Kim's head to keep from looking at the incision and blood. "Now this," Dr. Kim said as he lifted a big, pink organ out of the abdomen, "is the sigmoid colon." I was starting to feel sick. I had to keep telling myself, "You will not get sick. You will not get sick. You will not get sick." Dr. Kim pushed the sigmoid colon back into the abdominal cavity and pulled out a grey-colored thing that looked like a twisted rope. "And this," he said holding it aloft, "is the spermatic cord." At that point I left the room before Dr. Kim had another patient on the floor.

Once outside, I was all sweaty and felt nauseous, but I'm happy to report that I didn't faint or vomit. That was the end of my surgical internship. I know surgery is not for me, I don't even like to clean fish. I'm reminded of the painting *The Anatomy Lesson,* whenever I think back to Dr. Kim's operating room in Tororo.

With the TGS students back in school, our travels were over for a while. I was busy each day with teaching. Once each month, I had the evening and weekend "duty" responsibility that required that I be in the cafeteria for student meals and make sure that the students were in bed at 10 p.m. The schedule was arranged so that an American and an African teacher shared duty. Usually a man and a woman. That covered all the bases. A man, a woman—one African, one American.

At mealtimes, the students were assigned to tables. They came into the cafeteria and sat down in their assigned seats. The African cafeteria staff brought the food to the tables. The food was then ladled out onto each student's plate.

I was on duty one evening at dinnertime. The students had all entered the cafeteria and were seated at the tables. Everything seemed to be going on as usual, when one table of students started screaming. It was in the middle area of the cafeteria. "What's that all about," I asked the African teacher sharing duty with me? Before I could make my way to the table with the screaming girls, the entire cafeteria was screaming. It was like the waves of a stone that's thrown into a lake. The screaming radiated out and out in an ever-widening circle until the entire cafeteria was filled with screaming students who were jumping up and trying to run to the door. It was impossible to find out what had happened. Everyone was running and screaming. Chairs were overturned, food was spilled on the floor. What a mess! When it ended, I was left alone in the cafeteria, and 400 students were outside. I went outside and asked, "What happened?" Several voices answered my question, "A leezard has been cooked!" A "Leezard?" "What's a "leezard," I wondered? Oh, then I knew. The walls of the buildings had lizards on them, both inside and outside. There were big orange and black lizards, blue and black lizards, little white lizards—no big deal. They were all over. We never killed the lizards, I always figured they ate the bugs. But tonight, a lizard had been stewed and ladled out on a student's plate. It probably fell into the pot while the food was cooking and got stewed.

Now, this was a real problem. Four hundred girls missed a meal and refused to eat in the cafeteria. They said that one of the cooks had purposely stewed this lizard to poison them. There were all kinds of stories going around the school that night. Some students said it was an African from a hostile Kenyan tribe trying to kill them. Others said that this had been going on for a long time, and that is why they had not been feeling well. At any rate, the students were not going to eat in the cafeteria again.

The next day we had a faculty meeting; and it was decided that the Headmistress, Miss Roop, and other faculty members would eat their meals in the cafeteria to show the students that the food was not poison.

Actually, the cafeteria food wasn't bad. Pancakes, eggs, hot or cold cereal, and fruit were served at breakfast. The evening meal was usually a stew consisting of ground peanut stew over matoke (cooked banana) or a potato-like root, called cassava, with a cheese sauce. The only problem with meals were religious dietary laws. Some of the students' religion did not allow them to eat meat. Most of the students were allowed to eat eggs. We never had meat or fish. Protein was provided by beans, cheese, eggs, and peanuts. There were always plenty of fruit and vegetables.

After a week or so the cafeteria "leezard" was forgotten, and Miss Roop was able to eat her meals at home.

17

Mail was a very important part of the day for us. It provided the only contact we had with friends and family in the States. The mail from the States usually took eight or nine days to reach us and was eagerly looked forward to.

There were two sources of mail—our private post office box in town or mail through Tororo Girls School. All of our friends and relatives used the private post office box address. It was quicker. The mail that I received from University of Massachusetts, USAID, and the Embassy came to the TGS address.

I went to the post office in town just before lunch every day. That way I could read the mail as I ate lunch. By the time the TGS driver picked up the mail and delivered it back to the school to be sorted and put in the faculty mailboxes, it was always a day later. A day is very important when one is waiting for mail. We devoured every word of the letters we received from the States. I would read and then reread the mail and then read parts of it to the children. The mail that I picked up at noon was usually answered that day and sent out the next day.

We used air letter aerogram when writing home. These are a lightweight, single blue sheet with "fold along this line" flaps that seal in the message leaving the address on the outside. Greeting cards and sealed envelopes sometimes never made it. I am guessing that postal workers somewhere along the line took these for any money or

Town market in Toro.

valuables which they might contain. However, boxes did get delivered after given a long delay. We subscribed to *Newsweek* magazine which is printed on light-weight paper for overseas subscribers. These were even lighter when the Ugandan government censors cut out sections of the magazine that were "undesirable" for East African consumption. It was strange to receive *Newsweek* with sections cut out. Didn't the censors realize that we were listening to The Voice of America (in special English) and the BBC?

We knew that we had a package coming from my parents. We had asked them to send a pair of sneakers for each of the kids. They wrote and told us the date that they had shipped the parcel, so we were expecting it. When, after several weeks, it didn't arrive, I started asking the others at TGS how long packages took to arrive from the States. To my surprise, there were several Americans at TGS who had been waiting for packages that they knew had been shipped. Some of the staff had been waiting three and four months. I checked at the post office in Uganda and also had my parents ask in the States just how long it would take to receive parcels shipped from the States to Uganda. Both sides said approximately six weeks. I also learned that all parcels entered Uganda in Entebbe and were then shipped to Mbale where they were distributed to Tororo. Armed with this information, and accompanied by George Andrezejewski, I drove to the postal warehouse in Mbale, some twenty miles north of Tororo. It was a Saturday, and the post office would close at 1 p.m. so we arrived bright and early.

When we arrived at the warehouse, I told the African on duty that we were from Tororo Girls School and were going to look through the warehouse for our packages. I remember thinking that I was "taking over" just like Mary Riley had the day we arrived at the airport in Entebbe. I didn't "ask permission." I told the person what to do, and he did it. Amazing! By 1 p.m. George and I had found over 30 packages that were sitting in the warehouse addressed to Americans at TGS. I don't know why they hadn't been delivered. Some of them must have been in that warehouse several weeks. It may have been a language problem. Perhaps the postal workers at Mbale were not able to read English very well. There were not many English or American expatriates working in Mbale. Mbale had Chinese expatriates. The first "communists" that I had ever met in my life were these Chinese in Mbale.

I had seen these men working in Uganda. This Chinese "Peace Corps" was working in Tanzania, Kenya, and Uganda. In Tanzania they were building a railroad. A copy of the *East African Sunday Nation* carried a half-page picture of these men gathered in a circle with Africans holding little song books and singing a "revolutionary song." The caption read, "WORKERS' PLAYTIME—A REVOLUTIONARY SONG." The article said,

> The engineering and technical personnel of the Chinese railway survey team have cemented a close friendship with the Tanzanian workers, reports the official Chinese Hshinhua News Agency.
>
> The agency took this picture, somewhere in Tanzania, to illustrate how "together they spend a happy life despite hard work." It shows Tanzanian workers joining their Chinese colleagues in the singing of a "revolutionary song" at work break.
>
> China has agreed to finance the 1,000-mile Tanzanian-Zambia railway.

In Tanzania (to our south) the Chinese communists were building a railway. In Kenya (to our east) and in Uganda, itself, these Chinese were working on agricultural projects.

I had seen these Chinese young men standing up to their chest in swamp water building irrigation canals in Uganda. I wouldn't as much as put my toe in that water. These Chinese were standing in it up to their armpits digging up muck for irrigation ditches. How can they do that?—the snakes, the crocodiles, not to mention the disease. Someone once asked P.T. Barnum about his circus depiction of the Bible verse, "A lion shall lay down with a lamb." Barnum had a lion and a lamb in the same cage with this Bible verse overhead. "Well" said a observer, "it must take a lot of patience to accomplish that." "No, Mr. Barnum replied, "it takes a lot of lambs." I always thought it must take a lot of Chinese to accomplish the building of irrigation ditches in Uganda.

Uganda has a lot of acreage that is ideal for growing rice. I have been told that the marshes surrounding Lake Victoria and along the Nile River are well suited to rice production. It has been estimated that Uganda, if properly cultivated, could produce enough rice for all of East Africa. The Chinese were not only building rice paddies, they were building political allies in East Africa. The girls at TGS often wore little red pins with the bust of Chairman Mao or the Chinese communist flag on them.

I had always wanted to meet one of these Chinese, and I got my chance one day in Mbale. I went into a small grocery shop, and there before my very eyes was a "communist!" I had always thought that these Chinese must have been to language school before arriving in East Africa and probably spoke Swahili better than the Africans. So, I gave him a slight, oriental bow and, in my very best Swahili, said: "Habari Za Machana?" (How are you today?) To which he returned my bow and replied in English; "Yes, I am from China." He had mistaken my Swahili "Machana" for the English sound alike "from China." I was dumbfounded. He couldn't speak Swahili, but he spoke English! He probably had a doctorate from Harvard, or maybe he went to that California University, "UCRA."

The post office in Tororo not only had trouble delivering packages, it had problems with stamp supply. On more than one occasion I had tried to purchase Ugandan stamps from the Tororo Post Office only to be told that they had run out of stamps. What do you do in that case? You want to send a letter, but the post office has no stamps. "We don't sell stamps today, you must come back Tuesday, next week," I was told. Living and working in Africa takes a great deal of patience.

We drove up to the post office in Tororo one Sunday morning to get our mail. The post office boxes open from outside the building. So, one could check his box at any time of the day or night. This particular Sunday there were five or six men on the roof of the post office removing the tin sheeting. As I climbed the steps to the porch to get my mail, I said to these workers "Kazi Mingi." (Too much work) in reference to Sunday labor. They laughed, and replied "Mingi Sana, Bwana." (Very much, Sir.) The next day, Monday, I went to the post office, as I usually did, at noontime. There were several African men in business suits and policemen inside the post office. This was unusual for Tororo, so I asked one of these men what was happening. He told me the post office had been broken into, and they were investigating. To which I replied, "I was here yesterday, Sunday, and talked with some men who were working on the roof." The African in the business suit said, "Do you think these were the men who removed a section of the roof, entered the building, and stole the mail?" It was like talking to Sherlock Holmes. "Why, I never thought of that." I replied. "You may be right." He never saw the sarcasm in my reply. I wonder if he was correct? Brilliant!

18

"You must break this into small pieces, which must fall among the plants in your garden. When the wind and hail come, the plants will not be destroyed." A witch doctor in the local Tororo Town Market was telling me how to use the ostrich egg that I was inspecting from his collection of wares. "How much do you want for this egg," I asked? We, of course, bartered for the price of the egg and finally settled on five shillings, or approximately 70 cents, American. A bargain when I consider that I've seen ostrich eggs advertised in the *New Yorker* magazine for $75.

This egg, however, was not for wind and hail protection. It was a birthday gift for Phyllis Roop, our headmistress. I was going to have Theophilus Mazinga letter a birthday greeting on it. "Ted" was the African at TGS who taught art courses; and was very good with tie and dye fabrics, sculpture, oils, lettering—he did just about the whole thing in the arts. I washed this ostrich egg shell and Theophilus lettered it in "Old English" style the following:

HAPPY BIRTHDAY
To Phyllis Roop
(a good egg)

The perfect gift for "the person who has everything." I wonder if anyone else in the entire world has ever received an ostrich egg with a birthday greeting on it? Phyllis is a "good egg," and I knew that she would enjoy her birthday egg. One day, as I was returning from lunch, she called, "Coming back late from lunch again, Stewart?" To which I replied, "Phyllis, I don't think you love me any more, and you're my headmistress." She laughed and said, "I do too love you any more."

I had not come to Tororo Town Market for an ostrich egg for Phyllis. The thought of giving her this egg suggested itself to me as I walked by the witch doctor. He was always situated with his back to the west cement wall of the market. Perhaps he had more power when facing the east. Cameras were forbidden in the market area; but when I wanted to take some pictures, a five shilling note pressed into the palm of the Tororo Town Council guard took care of this. If I were to have brought a camera into the market, the African vendors would have started screaming at me and would probably have ripped the camera from my hands and perhaps beaten me. However, my five shilling "gratuity" provided me with the escort of a uniformed guard with the initials "TTC" (Tororo Town Council) emblazoned on his military jacket and a billy club in his hand.

Not only did my protector order the vendors to stand still for my photography, he posed with them. Well, not all of them. The witch doctor had some "mysterious" authority over this guard. Even after I had purchased my ostrich egg, the witch doctor refused my request for a picture. He said that photographs took some of his "power," and the guard motioned me on with this baton and the word, "Quenda." (Go)

The Tororo Town Market was about the size of a college basketball court, and is surrounded by a high cement wall with wooden buildings along the inside perimeter.

The floor was cement with several rows of corrugated tin roofs supported by tall, four-inch diameter, iron pipe. The vendors placed their wares on tables under these tin roofs. This protected against the equator's direct rays of the sun. On these tables were piles of cabbage, onions, tomatoes, bananas—cooking and sweet, fish, meat, eggs, chickens, and peanuts. I had come for peanuts and a bottle of peanut oil. The ostrich egg was an "impulse" purchase.

With these peanuts we provided ourselves with the peanut butter we couldn't find in Uganda's stores. We had a peanut butter recipe from a friend in the States—roast and grind the peanuts, add peanut oil, sugar, and salt. Stir this mess up, and put it in glass jars. Delicious! However, it did tend to separate, and had to be stirred before each use. I show my age when I confess that as a young child, growing up in New York State, this is the way peanut butter always was. The oil separated from the ground-up peanuts. This was the case until the wonder of "homogenized" peanut butter came along—just after we got "sliced bread" and "soap right in the Brillo pad." "Oh!" Grandma said, "What will they think of next." Well, whatever they "think of next," it will not be in Africa for a long time.

Roasting peanuts and making our own peanut butter was something we all enjoyed. We had the pleasures of the aroma of peanuts roasting in the kitchen; of mixing the peanut oil, salt, and sugar; and then of "tasting" to be sure that it was "just right." The kids loved cleaning the sides of the mixing bowls and "licking" all the spoons, table knives, and spatulas free of excess peanut butter. It was fun, and we did it our way—finger lickin' " good.

We also roasted our own coffee beans. A Dutch priest, Piet Molenaar, came to Tororo quite often. We all knew and enjoyed Father Molenaar. He worked with tribal people in a coffee-growing region, and sold their "green" coffee beans to us.

I could always tell when Father Molenaar had been around—our kitchen would have the "delicious" aroma of Mount Elgon coffee roasting.

Soon after I arrived from the States to start teaching at TGS, a European country gave Uganda foreign aid in the form of dairy equipment. This equipment consisted of stainless steel milk vats with a rotating paddle. With these milk vats, the Ugandan Government decided it would go into the dairy industry, thus, keeping the currency being spent by Ugandan residents for Kenya's milk. It didn't matter that the Uganda Milk Board did not have pasteurized milk from disease-free cows, that wasn't a concern. What mattered was that Uganda now had a new industry to help the economy. So, Mr. Patel at Tororo General Store no longer had Kenyan milk. We now had to purchase our milk, Ugandan milk, from the Tororo Town Market. Don Williams, our TGS business manager, said this was not a problem. USAID was going to give TGS faculty and staff milk pasteurizing machines. In fact, Don already had one in his home.

I went down to the Tororo Town Market to take a look at our new source of milk. Inside the market was one of these new stainless steel milk vats. It was plugged into the electric current and the paddle was slowly turning the new Uganda milk supply in a slow circle around the inside of the two-bathtub sized vat. The milk in the vat was being supplied by African men and women. While I was there, one African woman came in with what looked like an old wine bottle corked with a folded banana leaf. The operator poured her milk in the vat with the rest, paid the woman, and returned her bottle. I can only imagine the condition of this milk after it had been carried a few miles in the wine bottle, it was probably more cheese than milk. This milk was gently flowing around the vat carrying with it bits of grass, flies, and little dark brown pieces of some unknown substance. You put your money down, the vat operator filled the number of clear plastic bags requested, and the top of the bag was closed with a hot clamp that "sealed in the goodness," and the badness as well. Wonderful! We all went home and drew up a schedule of dates that each TGS faculty and staff member would make the trip to Nairobi for our milk. All except Don Williams.

Don was going to give the USAID pasteurizers a "go." Don, of course, was in a difficult position. The American Embassy had to support the efforts of the Ugandan government's milk industry. The Embassy put the pressure on Don Williams, as TGS business manager, to persuade the Americans at TGS to drink "local milk." We took a look at the milk Don's pasteurizer was producing, pinched our noses closed, and said "UUKKK!" The local milk went through Don's machine, and came out in a sour-smelling glop of curdle that I wouldn't feed my dog. I didn't have a dog, but I wouldn't even feed it to "Tokie," Bill Gatchell's dog.

George Andrezejewski and I had a new greeting. I would say, "George Andrezejewski drinks local milk!" To which George would reply, "With Gusto! Gusto Okello." "Okello" is an African name that is as common in Uganda as "Jones" is in the States. That was always followed by our "Jumbo Guano Kubwa" (Hello, you big bird shit.) greeting.

The Ugandan Government was very serious about its new milk industry. It was not wise to voice negative opinions about the quality of Uganda's milk. The following

Uganda Argus article hints that one could face legal problems if one complained about the milk.

ANGER AT MILK MALICE

A spokesman for the Dairy Industry Corporation said last night that malicious allegations had been made about the quality of Uganda milk.

He said Uganda milk has been known to be of higher quality than any other type of milk consumed in Uganda, but in some cases it had been adulterated in order to give a false impression to some members of the public that Uganda milk was not good.

He warned that anyone making allegations in the future would be called upon to give evidence to support his statement or court action would be taken by the Corporation against him.

Shortly after this, a letter to the editor had the following comment:

I note correspondence in your columns of June 21 about the quality of milk, together with a threat by the Dairy Industry Corporation on critics.

Without commenting on the outlook of a public body which is so sensitive to criticism as this, I wonder exactly how quality is defined in the case of milk. I, myself, would hesitate to grade milk, not being an expert, but I have noticed that in recent weeks milk poured into my breakfast coffee changes the color of my black coffee to muddy grey. Previously, I have been accustomed to my coffee being a cheerful coffee-brown color.

I wonder if the spokesman for the Dairy Industry Corporation would like to comment on this. Yozefu. Masaka, Uganda.

The Tororo Town Market was still a good source of fresh vegetables, fruits, and peanuts. However, we left the local milk alone. We shared our milk runs to Nairobi, and when this supply would run short, we had powdered milk from Holland. We purchased 50 pounds of powdered Holland milk. It didn't have a lowered fat content like skim milk, and was a suitable substitute for Kenya milk.

Things could be "touch and go" in the market as well. One day while I was purchasing our fresh vegetable and fruit supply, I heard a commotion at the gate followed by several men and women running and climbing over the walls to escape. "What's happening?" I asked an African vendor. "It's the Army." He replied. About that time, I saw several soldiers with rifles spread through the market grabbing people and hauling them out the front gate to an awaiting military-style truck. I didn't know what was going on, but I wasn't too concerned. It seemed like a local problem. Hey, I'm an American. I've got my passport. I thought it was about time I went home, so I started toward the gate. Wrong thing to do. It looked as though I was trying to escape. I guess I was.

As I retreated though the gate to the safety of my trusty VW van, I had to pass by some soldiers. I politely nodded my head and said "Jambo." To which a soldier said "Chit!" "Chit?" Whatever happened to "Port!" Well, maybe he means "Port." So, I said, "I have my passport at home. I'll go and get it if you need to see it." The soldier said, "No passport, Chit." I started to get my old, familiar "Senegal feeling" again. I didn't want to be "cracked" over the head and thrown in that military van like some of these African people were. "What is a 'Chit,'" I asked. The soldier's English was not good and I didn't trust my Swahili to carry this situation off, so I stuck with English. Another soldier came over and said "You must show your chit for your poll tax." "Poll Tax," I replied, "I don't even vote here." "Then you are a tourist?" The soldier said. "No, I am not a tourist, I live here." I explained. "If you live here, you must pay poll tax and show us your chit." He said.

Well, I thought I was going in the truck. But after a long discussion with the soldiers, during which time a large crowd of Africans had gathered around us, I went off to the local police station in my VW with what seemed to be the "Military Type" who was in charge of this "Chit Review."

We arrived at the police station and I was allowed to call TGS. I called Don Williams. "Hey, Don, you better get down to the police station and bail my butt out of here. The army wants to take me to prison in a truck." We waited for Don to arrive. "He will be here in just a few minutes. We must wait here. We must not leave here." I told the soldier. I didn't know where the prison was that the truck was going to, and I didn't care to find out. I needed to wait for Don Williams.

As I waited in the one-room police station with the soldier, I saw several men sitting on the floor. They were all Africans and were united by a "common bond"—their ankles were secured with an iron chain. There must have been a dozen or so of these men on this one chain. They were sitting on the floor having their meal. A large metal basin, much like the ones I had seen used for washing clothes in Uganda, contained three large cooked fish. These prisoners were sitting on the floor all reaching into the basin picking out pieces of fish. One man picked out a fish head and sucked on it for a while. When he had finished, he dropped the head back into the basin. Then, a second man picked up that same fish head, looked it over and sucked on it for something the first man had missed. Dirty hands reached into the "community basin," picked out fish bones, sucked the meat off the bone and tossed it back into the basin. It was like watching dogs chewing on bones. *Bon appetit!*

Just as the meal was finishing, Don Williams came into the police station, and gave a paper to the soldier in charge. The soldier laughed and allowed me to leave with Don Williams. Things in Africa can change so quickly. One minute everything is fine and the next minute you are in real bad trouble. On the way back to TGS Don said, "Oh, don't worry, they would have only had you for a day or two and then we would have found out where you were and gotten you back. You worry too much." Oh, go drink your local milk with gusto! I thought. Don Williams always thought that the rest of us let "little things" bother us too much. Bill Gatchell compared Don to "The Wizard of Oz." "Don has the answer to all our problems." Bill would say. "Just follow the 'Yellow Brick Road' up to Wizard William's house." We're off to see the Wizard, the wonderful Wizard of TGS—follow the yellow brick road, follow the yellow brick road, follow the yellow brick road.

19

It didn't seem possible to us, but we were in the second semester at Tororo Girls School. A lot had happened in the last few months. My thoughts went back to reading the ad, "Teach Business Subjects in East Africa," Doubleday, the flight over, and the "Port" episode in Senegal. We had all grown. John didn't wear diapers, or wet the bed. He was so proud of that. Stephen had lost some teeth. Paula and Beth were the "darlings" of the TGS girls. No other family had girls. The Andrezejewskis had Alyessia, but she was too young to roam the TGS campus as Paula and Beth did. The African students just loved them. We had seen "The elephants, the zebra, the lions, the giraffe!" and a whole lot more. We had also found some new friends, the Gatchells and the Andrezejewskis had been a lot of help to us. Whenever we felt homesick, we would just visit with George and Joan or Bill and Ellen, and it would pass. Then, too, their children taught our children how to play centipede hockey.

Now we were going to lose the Gatchells. They were ending their tour and were going to return home to Massachusetts. Andrezejewskis were at TGS when we arrived, and they would be there when we left. I knew I would have to return to SUNY at the end of the initial two-year assignment. If I signed on for another two years, I would not have a job waiting for me.

Bill had taught math at the secondary-level in Massachusetts, and he would be going back to his job in Wilbraham. Gatchells were looking forward to getting back to the States and had a great return trip planned. Ellen Gatchell had relatives living in Norway. They were going to fly from Uganda to Oslo and spend some time in Norway with Ellen's family. What an opportunity! Ellen had kept in contact with her Norwegian relatives, but had never had a chance to visit them. Now, with USAID paying for the return, they would be able to do it. School would be over at TGS in June, and they would have the summer in Norway before returning to their home in Massachusetts.

Then they got the bad news. The United States Government had a change of policy. Americans working for USAID would have to do all their traveling on US carriers. As long as USAID was paying for travel, it was going to be on American carriers. This was an attempt to keep American dollars in American hands. There were no American carriers going to Norway from East Africa. The Gatchells would get on the plane in East Africa, and step out of the plane in the USA. *Bon Voyage!* Gatchell was mad, Gatchell was furious, Gatchell was moved to write a poem.

I was in my yard, when I heard Gatchell yell, "Hey, Bill, come 'ere: I got something to read to you." I walked over to the wire fence separating our yards. Gatchell produced a paper, from which he read:

OUR GOVERNMENT
by Bill Gatchell

Our Government is like a bird winging through the sky.
Oblivious to us below, it dumps within our eye.
I'd like to hunt our government, and when I saw it pass
I'd load my gun with number aught, and shoot it in the
    A. I. D.

    Fantastic! I loved it. That's a healthy expression of anger. This wasn't the first poem that had been written out of frustration at things we could not change at TGS. "Lord grant me the power to change the things I can change, and write poems about the things I can not change." A good rule to live by.
    About the time the British seemed to be blocking every attempt we made to prepare the TGS students for the Overseas Cambridge Examination, I wrote the following:

TGS AT THE BAT
by Bill Stewart

The outlook wasn't very bright for TGS that day.
For half the faculty were new with the Cambridge on
    the way.
USAID didn't understand how the girls would do so bad.
U. of Mass didn't seem to care, and that's what made us
    mad.
Poor Elwyn, he'd been stored away in an old, abandoned
    shack;
while Allen fired a few more profs, just to get them off
    his back

The faculty was tried and true, but well-nigh worn away,
with leaking roofs, rancid milk, and killing snakes all day.
So, Riley took to pambi, and Gatchell flew on home.
Stewart's goatee had grown so long, you could part it with a comb.
Roop was sleeping afternoons, the Ugandans were chasing men.
Williams hadn't paid poll tax, so they threw him in the pen.
George was in the courts all day, as he was being sued.
The students all had gotten sick, for a lizard had been stewed.
But then the news that saved our necks fell on our weary ear
AID changed the school to a brewery, and we starting making beer.

There are some things that have to be explained in order to understand that poem. "Riley took to pambi." Pambi is a native beer. "Stewart's goatee" USAID said American men must be clean shaven, so I grew a beard. "Elwyn—in an old abandoned shack" There was a new administrator at U. Mass who was not treating the Uganda Project with anything but contempt. His name is Dwight Allen and, in my opinion, he is the "Bubonic Plague of Education." I feel sorry for the institution that has Allen on its faculty or administration. He is no longer at U. Mass. "George was in the courts all day. . . ." This was a joke that George had spoken too loud and too often about the Uganda Milk Supply. That explains all the "in parts" of this poem. The line concerning Roop and Ugandans has no meaning, it was just needed to fill the proper rhythm of the poem. The rest you will understand from the previous chapters.

There is one more poem that I remember concerning a trip that Bill Gatchell and I took to pick up the Calvert School courses I had ordered for Stephen and Paula.

The Asian school was sufficient for Beth, who was first grade level in the States. John started kindergarten in January, and the Asian school would meet his needs. However, with Paula in second grade, and Stephen in third grade, we needed something more in line with what they would be doing in New York. So, we ordered these grade level courses from the Calvert School in the States.

The courses had arrived, and Bill Gatchell offered to drive me to Entebbe to pick them up at the airport. I wanted to pick them up at the airport to make sure I got them. The drive to Entebbe was a straight run on the main road through Kampala. It was the road we had taken that first "homesick" day when we had just arrived in Uganda.

The trip was uneventful through Jinja and across Owen Falls Dam. It was, as usual, a bright, sunny day, and there was not a lot of traffic on the road. Just a normal day. Things were different after Owen Falls Dam. We came to a barrier across the road that had a big arrow pointing left and said DIVERSION, which is the British term for "Detour." The road was closed for some reason. We turned left onto a red, dirt road; which the British call "Murram." This mirram road ran through a sugarcane plantation. The red dust on this road was very bad. When we passed oncoming trucks and cars, we were engulfed in clouds of red dust. Having the windows closed didn't help much. This red powder covered everything in the car, including Bill and me. The diversion went on for miles and miles through sugarcane and irrigation ditches. We must have been on this mirram road a half hour when the car just stopped. We rolled to a halt with nothing around us but sugarcane—miles from a town. We just sat in the car looking at each other. What do we do now? Bill opened the rear door to inspect the engine. He had a VW bug and so the engine was in the back. After what seemed like a long time, Bill said, "I think the distributor rotor is gone. See this crack in the rotor? Well, that's the problem." "What are we going to do?" I asked. "There's a VW garage in Jinja. We could try that." Bill answered. "Jinja is miles back through this sugar cane." I said. "Well, that's what has to be done. However, we can't leave the car, or someone is going to go off with it, or, at very least, take parts from it. If we leave it, it won't be here when we come back. I'll stay with the car. You'll have to go back to Jinja." Bill said. "Walk all those miles?" I asked. "It's not that far." Bill said. "You've got to do it.

So, back down the diversion I walked, rotor in hand, headed for Jinja. I had only walked a mile or so, when I heard some vehicle coming behind me. It was, of all things, a bus. There was a bus coming! I could get a ride.

I flagged the bus down, climbed aboard, and off I went to Jinja. The bus was crowded with Africans. There were bicycles, chickens, and big bunches of bananas on top, but the ride was not half bad, considering the alternative. However, the bus driver kept stopping when we came upon Africans selling things at road-side stands. The driver would stop the bus, get out, and start bartering with the vendors. It would go on and on until some of the people on the bus would also get out and start arguing with the driver and/or vendors. This happened two or three times during the trip back to Jinja. The strange thing about it was that the driver never purchased anything. He was just stopping to argue. I had read about this in the newspaper. One letter to the editor of the *Uganda Argus* said,

> The habit which the bus drivers, conductors, and turn-boys have invented of delaying on the way for their own sake seems to cause much anger to the passengers who wish to reach their destinations quickly.
>
> When they come across goods being sold on the way such as oranges, bananas, etc., they stop the bus and involve themselves in long, unnecessary arguments with the sellers. They bargain for such a long time that the passengers get disgusted.
>
> People working for the public should not let it suffer for their own sake, or else if the service they offer is marred so simply, the public might boycott those concerned. Bus workers in the villages are experts in this though it will still not be unusual for even those working on major roads.
>
> If the bus officials neglect to look into this problem then the popularity of busses will be ruined and consequently the business will fail. Peter W. Bageya, Iganga.

My favorite newspaper article about bus transportation was from the *Kenya Daily Nation.*

THE THINGS THAT HAPPEN ON BUSES

Oh, the strange things that happen on the Kenya buses. Take the case of Mr. K. N. Karuri, of Limuru, for example.

There he was, a passenger on a vehicle run by Rukubi Bus Service and driven by Mr. J. K. Njuguna from Limuru to Nairobi. He expected to arrive on time, but then . . .

Near Mama Ngina Primary School in Kikuyu, the bus was stopped by the police. They wanted to charge the driver for not obeying the bus time-table, said Mr. Karuri.

The police wanted the driver to tell them the meaning of his initials "J.K." The driver declined to do so, and said the man who issued the license was not a fool, according to Mr. Karuri. After they had argued thus for about an hour, the passengers began to get restless.

"The passengers had paid their fares and they expected to be delivered to their destination on time." Mr. Karuri complained. Eventually the police took away the driver's license, and the driver decided to carry on without it.

Oh, the things that happen on the buses.

We completed the diversion stretch of the trip, got on the tarmac, crossed Owen Falls Dam, and there we were in Jinja.

It wasn't hard to find the VW garage in Jinja. It's a very small town with just a few buildings. Not only was I able to get the part for the VW, but I was able to talk them into sending me back with one of their mechanics to get Bill's car running again. Terrific! Back down the road, across the dam, and down the diversion to Bill and his VW bug. As we approached Bill's car, I could see about 10 or 15 African people standing around his car looking through the window at Bill. He was sitting in the driver's seat reading a paperback.

The mechanic fixed the car, and we were on our way to Entebbe for the Calvert courses. By the time we had gotten to the airport, picked up the Calvert courses, and returned back across the diversion we were tired, hot, and a dusty-red color from the mirram. It was on the way back through the diversion that Bill and I composed this poem. It is actually "The Star Spangled Banner" tune with these new words:

Oh say can you see, all the mirram on me?
We've traveled afar, over many di-ver-sions.
The windscreen has gone as we traveled along,
and the dudus are now plastered over our brow.
Oh, say, is that tarmac ahead of us now, Jack?
Or, must we forebear this mirram-clogged air?

That poem needs a couple of words explained. "Windscreen" is the British word for "windshield." "Dudu" is the Swahili word for "bug."

That's the complete reading of African Poems by TGS faculty. These poems are the result of frustration and not being able to do a thing about the situation but laugh.

The Gatchells were leaving, but, little did I know that my family would be back in the States without me before the Gatchells even left Uganda.

20

Many of the TGS faculty were going home. Riley was going. The Gatchells were going. Ruth Hepple, the science/biology teacher, was going. Williams was going. Helen Harms, the TGS music teacher, was going.

It seemed that I hardly knew the single women at TGS. They pretty much stayed together. Mary Riley taught the English classes. I had seen her around the school, and I knew that she lived in one of the apartments on the TGS campus, but I couldn't tell you which one. She had been the person who met us at Entebbe Airport when we first arrived. I saw the single women teachers at faculty meetings, but the only "social" occasion I remember seeing them at was when Uganda's President, Dr. Milton Obote, visited the school. President Obote, some members of the Ugandan Ministry, and Americans from USAID were given a tour of Tororo Girls School, sung to by the TGS choir, and treated to complimentary speeches about each other. The AID speeches congratulated President Obote and the Ministers of Parliament for the fine job they were doing in bringing education and a higher standard of living to the people of Uganda. The words "Democracy" and "Freedom" were sprinkled liberally in these speeches. President Obote's speech lauded the benevolence of the United States and expressed the expectation that such philanthropy would continue to ensure Uganda's future course.

What I got from all this oratory was that USAID was telling Obote, "You better give your people democracy, or our AID programs will dry up." While Obote was telling USAID, "You better keep the dollars flowing, or there will be more Chinese restaurants opening in Kampala."

Nothing was mentioned about the Uganda Democratic Party members being held in detention, Uganda's King Freddie in exile in England, or the fact that the Ugandan people had never voted Milton Obote to power. I guess that wasn't important.

President Obote's visit ended with a dinner. It consisted of a fruit course, cheese course, salad course, fish course, poultry course, beef course, desert, a wine with dinner, a wine with dessert, an after-dinner drink, coffee . . . it went on long after the sun had gone down. In fact, President Obote said it was the longest dinner he had ever attended. That made two of us.

The dinner was followed by dancing and an open bar. During the after-dinner period; USAID, Obote, his ministers, and the TGS faculty had the chance to talk with one another. Dr. Obote is very casual and easy to talk with. I walked over to him, shook his hand, and talked with him just as I would an old friend. He asked me what part of the States I was from, and we talked about my work at TGS and his work as president of Uganda. He said the best part of his work was the dinners, and the worst part was dealing with Ministers of Parliament in Kampala. He had the answer to that. If they disagreed with him, he just put them in detention.

However, Dr. Obote was not going to have the option of putting his political foes in detention much longer. Just as he had driven King Freddie out of Uganda and taken over as president, he would be driven out as well. It was going to happen three years after the evening we had talked together at The Rock hotel.

On January 26, 1971 *The New York Times* had the following article:

> Kampala, Uganda. Tuesday, January 26.
>
> Uganda's army ousted President Milton Obote yesterday and set up a military government.
>
> Thousands of cheering Ugandans thronged the streets of this East African capital celebrating the army take-over, while the President himself was still heading home after attending the Conference of Commonwealth Leaders in Singapore. . . .
>
> The new leader in Uganda is Maj. Gen. Idi Amin who rose from private to become commander of the army and air force and who will now head the military government.
>
> The first act of the new Ugandan leader was to order the release of all political prisoners detained by the Obote Government including five former cabinet ministers.

George Andrezejewski accidentally knocked a liter of beer off a table. As it went crashing to the floor, Bill Gatchell yelled from across the room, "Way to go, George!" Gatchell never missed an opportunity to extend his congratulations on the accomplishments of others. If looks could kill, Gatchell would have been shipped back to Massachusetts in a body bag that evening.

I knew Dr. Ruth Hepple a little better than Helen Harms or Mary Riley. That was because she taught science/biology and had a connection with George Andrezejewski, who also taught science classes. Ruth was a woman who had some definite opinions and was not afraid to voice them.

The year before we arrived in Uganda, Doubleday had to settle a dispute between Ruth and a woman named

Marion Balboni. I am not sure just what it was all about. Elwyn told me he had flown from U. Mass to TGS and found Balboni and Hepple ready to "strangle each other." He said he talked to these two women for hours. Finally, they shook hands and said they would let "bygones be bygones." However, as they were walking out the door, Ruth said, "You know, Marion, I never really felt you treated me right." With that the argument started all over again. Balboni left Tororo, and Hepple stayed on for another two years. When Balboni left, Phyllis Roop took her place as "headmistress."

Ruth was kind of an "odd duck." She had taken a trip to an East African game park and invited several of us over to her house—she lived in a house TGS rented in Tororo—to see some "fantastic" 35 mm slides she had taken of lions. The pictures were all out of focus. She wore glasses, but always took her glasses off when she looked through the viewfinder of the camera. She said she couldn't see through the viewfinder with her glasses on. Consequently, the pictures looked out of focus to me. She gave a commentary as we were watching the slides, never mentioning that they were out of focus. I wonder if her glasses corrected the fuzzy pictures we were viewing. She had her glasses off when she took the pictures. Now, with her glasses on, she may have been seeing them perfectly. The pictures were of two lions copulating—a lot of pictures, rolls of pictures. "Now, there you see the male lion on top of the female lion." Hepple's commentary went. "See how the female is turning her head snarling at the male." Several pictures of the "snarl." "Now, see how the male arches his back. See that?" Several pictures of the "arch." "Now, they are resting. See the male lie on his back. See them resting?" Several "resting" pictures. "They were like that for about an hour. I had the safari driver park the car for the entire afternoon. By the time it was evening, they had mated four times." Hepple continued her commentary, "Now, this is an hour later. See the male lion on top of the female lion. . . ." This slide show went on and on. Ruth was really into biology. I wonder what the African safari driver thought as he sat in his Land Rover all afternoon while a European woman took pictures of lions screwing?

The Williams were leaving. Don and Jackie Williams had three boys, all under ten years old. Don was busy in Kampala a lot. He was the business manager and dealt with the Ugandan Government, USAID, the Embassy, and U. Mass. He was the person we ordered our supplies, etc. through. As business manager, he had to try to keep USAID happy and keep the TGS faculty happy as well. This was not always easy to do. Take for example the "local milk" business. USAID and the Embassy wanted to look good in the eyes of the Ugandan Government by being supportive of their new milk industry. So, they decided the Americans at TGS were going to drink the local milk. They supplied us with the pasteurizers. We weren't having any part of it. Don was in the middle. Did the USAID and Embassy people drink local milk? Guess again. They had fresh vegetables and dairy products flown in on air force jets from West Germany. Don Williams had the "pain in the neck" part of the project. As a result, he kept pretty much to himself. If USAID had any bad news for us, it filtered down through our business manager.

I visited the Williamses at their home in Arizona once after we returned to the States. They were living in Apache Junction, just east of Phoenix near the Superstition Mountains. Their oldest son disappeared after they returned to Arizona. The boy was a teenager. He left home to go hunting one day and never returned. The police used dogs to trace his scent. The dogs traced the boy's trail through the Superstition Mountains to a road where the trail ended. It is assumed that he got into a car. That was the end of it. Nothing. Just gone.

It was June, and TGS had a month of classes left in the school year. Phyllis Roop had temporarily returned to the States. She had been called back to U. Mass to interview the candidates for next year's open positions at TGS and to talk with USAID in Washington. She would be gone about a month.

Phyllis was the best "boss" I ever had. We trusted her, and felt that she was "on our side." Phyllis cared about us and what we needed. She wasn't the "company" person, she was more like a union representative. I always thought she was trying to help me: and I would, in return, give her my total support.

Phyllis and I signed on to the Uganda Project at the same time. She was from the Denver area of Colorado, where she had been the supervising principal of a large school district which included both elementary and secondary schools. She was a very able administrator. What people liked about Phyllis was her perfect combination of professional ability and personal care for the people she worked with. Phyllis was an attractive, 5' 10" tall woman in her mid-thirties. She had never married. She had been engaged to a pilot who had died while in the service. After her fiancé's death, she concentrated on her career, and, as I've said, she was the best "boss" I ever worked for.

Working for USAID was like swimming in shark-infested waters. USAID didn't care about Bill Stewart, or Bill Gatchell, or George Andrezejewski. We were expendable to them. It was "the budget" or their own promotion up through the ranks that they cared about.

After all, I was only in the Uganda Project for two years. There had been others before me, and there would be others after me. I was too expensive—passports, physical examinations, airfare, school fees—four children and two adults. The embassy people and the USAID people were career people; TGS faculty and staff, and Peace Corps people were just adventurers "having a good time." Maybe that was true. I wasn't going to spend my life in foreign service and didn't care about climbing up the promotion ladder. However, we depended on the American Embassy to take care of us in Uganda. We were in the trenches for their projects. The Uganda Project was a "feather" in someone's cap, and we at TGS were the horses who were pulling this project along. I was soon to find out just how much I could depend on USAID in an emergency.

It was sudden. We went to bed one night, and I woke up the next morning with a very sick wife. Just like that. Joyce had not slept well that night. She had been up two or three times vomiting and had severe abdominal pain. The next morning her skin was yellow looking, and she was in a lot of pain. She had tried standing, sitting, lying on her back, laying on her stomach, doubled over, stretched out. Nothing relieved her pain—aspirin, antacids, milk, water—nothing.

I went to town and got one of the British doctors to come back to the house with me. He looked at the color of Joyce's skin and said, "Your wife has hepatitis. I can tell by the color of her skin." "What do you mean, 'hepatitis,' we're taking gamma globulin every six months—massive shots of GG. It can't be hepatitis," I replied. "Well, that's what it is whether you take GG or not." He said in an "I'm the doctor here" voice. "I'm going to give you something for the pain and you'll be able to sleep. Since your husband tells me you're a nurse, I am going to leave this Pethidine here for you to take as needed. I believe you Americans call this 'Demerol.' I am leaving directions for the amount." With that he left and said he would be back the next day.

That day Joyce slept between shots of Demerol, while I taught my classes. Beth and John went off to the Asian school. Stephen and Paula read their Calvert course materials. The next day Joyce wasn't better. She still had a lot of pain, and her skin was an even deeper yellow. The doctor came back, looked at his patient, pronounced himself correct in his original diagnosis, and left more Demerol.

Stephen came home from Gatchells crying. "Mr. Gatchell told me that I'm not allowed to come to their house until my mother gets over her hepatitis," Stephen sobbed. "Well, Stephen," I said, "You have to remember that the Gatchells are going home, and they don't want to get sick now. Mr. Gatchell isn't being mean to you. He's just trying to keep his family healthy." We felt like lepers. I should probably have stood in front of the door and yelled, "UNCLEAN! UNCLEAN!" if someone approached.

After three days of this pain and yellow skin, I decided it was time to get a second opinion. Does hepatitis cause so much pain? What about the GG shots we had been taking? We were careful to soak our fruits and vegetables in an antibacterial solution and to boil and filter our water. This can't be hepatitis. Can it?

We had heard of a doctor in Kampala. Sir H.E. Godfrey, I was told that he had been knighted by the Queen of England for his work in the colony, when Uganda was a colony. He had the reputation of being a very good doctor. So, off we went to Kampala to see Dr. Godfrey. There was no waiting. We had called ahead, and he knew that Joyce was in a lot of pain.

Dr. Godfrey examined Joyce and said, "I don't think this is hepatitis; but, just to be sure, I want to take some X-rays." He had X-ray equipment in his office. Within minutes he told us that Joyce did not have hepatitis. She had a large stone blocking the duct of her gallbladder, thus, the pain and the yellow skin. "I knew it wasn't hepatitis!" I exclaimed.

It was a relief to know that Joyce didn't have hepatitis, but now we had another problem. The stone was lodged in the duct and she would have to have surgery soon. Uganda had the New Mulago Hospital in Kampala. The building was very modern looking from the outside. However, patient care wasn't good. Dr. Godfrey told us my wife should return to the States, immediately. She had to have her gallbladder removed, and he advised against having it done in Uganda. Godfrey was the only British doctor in Kampala. He wasn't a surgeon and could not recommend anyone at all. "You'll just have to get her back to America." He said. "That's all there is to it. I know Ambassador Stebbins and your USAID Director, Will Muller. I'm sure they will agree. I'll give you a letter to give to them recommending that your wife return to America for this surgery. Wait for the letter, and take it with you today. We don't want to waste any time on this." We left Dr. Godfrey's office and drove to the Grand Hotel. We were going to be in Kampala at least one night.

Bright and early the next morning I got up, showered, had breakfast, and went off to meet with Will Muller at USAID, Kampala. I had the feeling that "good ole Will" was going to fight every attempt that I made to send Joyce and the children back to the States for her surgery. I wasn't disappointed. At first, Muller would not hear of my wife leaving Uganda for an operation, he said that there was a perfectly fine medical facility in Kampala. I showed him a copy of Dr. Godfrey's letter. "I can't believe Dr. Godfrey would write such a letter about this fine hospital." Muller said. "Fine hospital?" I bellowed. "Read the letter. Godfrey says it stinks! He recommends that my wife return immediately to the States for this surgery. Right here in the letter, read it, Mr. Muller." After a hour or so of arguing, Will Muller said he would allow my wife and the youngest child, John, to return. The other three children must stay with me in Uganda. Well, I had won one round, now I had to go another round to get the three other children back.

This went on for another two hours. I tried to compromise with Muller. We had a "rest and relaxation" provision in the contract which gave us a trip to Europe after one year at TGS. I told Muller I would give up this R&R if he would send all four children back to the States with Joyce. "You have to pay for airfare to England for all six of us." I said. "You can have that back, I won't take an R&R, and you'll save six tickets. You keep the R&R, just send my wife and children back to the States." "Oh, no, no, no, we can't do that." Will said. "That's part of your contract, that can't be changed. We'll send you to Europe. We will not, under any circumstances, send all four children back to the States with your wife." This went on for a while, and I finally gave up on Muller. I decided I would go to Phyllis for help. Will Muller and I had a bitter morning together, after which time, I left and sent a telegram to Phyllis Roop c/o U. Mass. Then we drove back to Tororo and waited to hear from the States. We received a telegram from Phyllis three days later. It read:

PERMIT ALL FOUR CHILDREN TO RETURN WITH MOTHER TO THE STATES. BEST WISHES FOR A SAFE JOURNEY, ROOP & ELYWN.

That's my headmistress! I thought she didn't love me anymore. She does too love me anymore. That is the kind of boss Phyllis was. I wrote her the following letter:

Dear Phyllis:
Thank you for all you have done in getting my wife and children home. I sure wish that you had been here to give me advice.

As you know, I went to Kampala to plead my case before USAID. I must say that I have never been so disappointed in all my life. Muller and I had a real "blow." It lasted three-and-one-half hours, and I was completely exhausted in the end. I tried every means possible to get Joyce and the children home. I went so far as to tell him that he could even take away my R&R if he would let them go. He said that this was impossible.

Now they are singing an entirely different tune. Since your cable came, Muller & Company are all humanitarian. They sent Dr. Adams up here to smooth things over and tell me just how desperately they are working to get my "poor" family home. But, the big catch is this. Now they tell me that they were doing this in the light of my offer to give up the R&R. So, kindly, old Dr. Adams has squeezed a promise out of me not to take an R&R. I tried to get him to wait till I talked to you, but he would not.

To tell the truth, I think that USAID is the worst organization that I have ever had the displeasure of working with. They don't care about us. All they care about is their budget.

I am 8,000 miles away from Massachusetts and can't really tell what is going on. I am convinced that you can not believe one word that AID says. This, however, is how I see things:

1. Muller was "dead set" against my wife and children

going home; but finally had to concede at least Joyce and the youngest.
2. He turned down my original offer to forego my R&R in order to get my family home.
3. Then you go to bat for us and get the kids home with Joyce, independent and contrary to USAID's wishes.
4. Muller finds out that his recommendations have been overruled, and sends Dr. Adams here on a pretence of trying to be helpful to us; and at the same time try to make me believe that it was all the philanthropic "heart of gold" of Muller. This, of course, gave them the opportunity of putting before me my original offer (which Muller had turned down) of giving up my R&R.

I think that the whole thing is a "rotten deal." I have agreed to forego the R&R on a "gentleman's agreement" basis. In my opinion, there was only "one" gentleman acting in the agreement. At least I can walk past USAID with my head up. The sooner I am done with USAID the better. In fact, I wish they would fire me, and I would be free from this "whole damn mess."

Anyway, I want to thank you for your help. I know it was because of you that Joyce and the children are coming home. I want to say that you are the best "boss" I have ever had. If I were you I would "get out" now and do something useful. This project is just one, big "fouled-up mess." Give my regards to Elwyn and his family.
Sincerely, Bill Stewart

So, there it was. We packed up the luggage, left Tororo, and headed to the airport at Entebbe. I gave everyone a big kiṣs, SMMAAKK, and a hug, and said "goodbye." This time Paula wasn't crying. She was happy to be going home to see her grandparents. We were all happy. Thank you, Phyllis.

21

It was very quiet at TGS. The students had gone back to their villages, the Gatchells were in Massachusetts. Hepple had gone home. Williams were back in Arizona. Roop was in the States. Andrezejewskis were on R&R, as were most of the other American faculty and staff. I guess I was left "holding the fort." Just Tokie and me. "Tokie" is the Swahili word for "one banana." She was the Gatchells' Alsatian dog. Gatchells had inherited Tokie from an American woman who had left after Gatchell's first year. I don't know how long Tokie had been around TGS, but she was old. She was nearly blind, couldn't hear well, and was getting unsteady on her feet. The worst thing about Tokie was that she "farted" a lot. I can remember Bill pushing the dog out the door, saying "TOKIE! My God, you stink! Get outside!" I had heard that often. So, there we were—"Farting Tokie" and me.

The house in town that Hepple had lived in was empty. I wanted that house. If Williams had been at TGS, I wouldn't have gotten it. However, Williams was gone, and, if I worked fast, I could get it before new people came to TGS and moved in. The house was in a suburban section of Tororo and was a "real" house. The houses on the TGS campus were like motel rooms—no character. The faculty houses were identical with two sections separated by a patio/breezeway. The yards were big, but were next to the "bush." Just down the road from the houses were banana trees and a native village. These villages were so close to the faculty houses that we could hear screaming at night if someone died in the village. There were also a lot of snakes—cobras, three-steppers, mambas, and the occasional python—"kubwa sana" (very big). In fact, I have a newspaper clipping showing four African men holding a huge python which had attacked one of a European's two German police dogs. The caption read:

MAN AND DOGS WIN BATTLE WITH PYTHON

A European living in Tororo won a single-handed battle with a 14-foot python which had attacked his dog.

The man, who did not want his name to be revealed, was walking in a forest area near Tororo with his two Alsatian dogs.

One of the dogs, which was about 50 yards ahead, was attacked by the python. The python wrapped itself around the dog. Within seconds, the dog was gasping for breath.

The man had no weapon and found that hitting the snake over the head with a stone had no effect. He grabbed the end of the snake's tail and tried to loosen its grip on the dog.

After leaving the dog the snake transferred its attention to the man. The Alsatian recovered and attacked the snake and was joined by the other dog which had been chasing baboons.

After a battle lasting half an hour, the man killed the snake by hitting it on the head with large rocks.

He said that it was interesting to see that the snake carried out its attack on the dog without first anchoring its tail around a tree or a bolder. Most people believe that pythons never attack in this way.

The snake attacked by biting, holding on with the

jaws and coiling itself around its victim. "Death must come very quickly" he said. He found the python's bite was quite severe, but it was not poisonous.

He advises people who walk in python country to carry a weapon—preferably a large knife.

Hepple's house was not close to a native village, and didn't have a snake problem. I'm sure that there were snakes around, but the houses were older, and were not close to the "bush." It looked like a house one might find in New York. It had a peaked, tile roof, which eliminated the "leaking roof" problem we had experienced on campus. I would not hear "HISS" at night and go searching for snakes. There were no wire fences between yards. The house had an attached garage, a front porch that ran the entire length of the house front, and nice front and back yards. There were lovely flower beds, a single banana tree, and an orange tree. The back yard was next to the Asian school that Beth and John attended. There would be no more driving to school. The kids would just walk out the back door, across the lawn, and into the school. They would also be able to eat their lunch at home. It was ideal.

There were nice neighbors. The Richters lived next door. They were an older German couple who had a daughter living in Kenya. Herr and Frau Richter came from Berlin. Prior to the Second World War, Herr Richter, didn't like what was happening in Germany. He was a pacifist and had a friend in the German government who told him that if he didn't leave Germany, he would be put in prison for his pacifist beliefs. Henry took an engineering job in the German colony of Tanzania, which was then called "Tanganyika." When the Second World War broke out, the British took over control of Tanganyika, which is surrounded by the former British colonies of Kenya and

Uganda. There was no fighting in Tanganyika, the Germans just sort of "gave up" Tanganyika to Britain. At the time of the British takeover, the Germans living in Tanganyika were given a choice by Britain. They could either become British citizens or be sent back to Germany. The Richters chose to become British citizens.

Herr Richter was an engineer; and after the war, he moved to Uganda to work in the cement plant at Tororo. They had been in Tororo since the early 50s. Frau Richter spent her days doing needlework and working in her flower garden. I believe she was a graduate of a German horticulture institute. Her flower garden reminded me of the Horticulture School at SUNY in Alfred. She knew what she was doing. On their travels through East Africa, Frau Richter collected exotic flowers and brought them back to her greenhouse.

Next to the Richters, lived Dr. Kim, the surgeon at Tororo Hospital. The Kims had several children. Richters raised flowers, Kims raised children.

I spent the last week in June moving into the house in town. I liked this house much better than the campus house. There were tile floors, not cement, a bookcase built into the wall, wooden door frames, and a porcelain kitchen sink in the kitchen. There were nice curtains on the windows, and a lovely front porch. It felt like "home." The TGS campus housing always felt like the Red Roof Inn.

The children would miss the Williams and Gatchell children when they returned. But, I knew they were going to like their new house. It just felt like "home."

There were two secondary schools in Tororo. TGS was for girls, the other school, Manjasi School, was operated by the Church of England for boys. Manjasi had a British faculty. Since they had male African students and we had female African students, there was not a feeling of "competition" between us. These British teachers were the "good guys" compared to the British "bad guys" that we had encountered in Kampala. We saw these people at The Tororo Club, and exchanged dinner invitations with them in our homes. Some of these British teachers were also leaving at the end of the school year. One man, David Thompson, had become our friend. He was from the extreme northern portion from Scotland. His father worked on a fishing boat that went into the North Sea, between Scotland and Norway. David had a Scottish accent, but we didn't have a problem understanding him. However, his father was another thing. David exchanged cassette tapes with his dad. One day David knocked at our door, portable tape recorder in hand. "Bill," David said, "I've brrat ye a tap of me faather fer yah to llisn ta. Ken yeh know what 'tis he's saaying." David played the tape. I could tell that it was a man talking, but it didn't sound like any language I had ever heard before. I couldn't understand a word of the tape, even after David translated for me and replayed the tape. "David, I kennay tel a werd." I said. It was just impossible for me to understand. His father lived in a fishing village on an island just off the northeast coast of Scotland.

David was returning to Scotland and asked if I would like to buy his motor scooter. It was an Italian Vespa. With the house in town, I would need transportation to TGS. I could ride the Vespa to school, leaving the car to Joyce for trips to the store, etc. So, I bought David's Vespa. The seat accommodated two riders, which meant I could give the children rides, one at a time. We were all set. We had a new house and were now a two-vehicle family. That's the American way! Oh, yes, one more thing. I bought a parrot. An African man came to the door of the house in town with an African Grey parrot. It was light grey with a splash of bright red feathers. I thought the kids would "love" the parrot, but after weeks of saying "pretty bird," all that parrot ever did was growl, try to bite our fingers, and eat red-hot chilies.

July Fourth was a special time for Americans living in Uganda. We all had been "summoned" to the American Embassy to observe the "Fourth of July" picnic. I really didn't want to drive to Kampala alone to have a picnic with Ambassador Stebbins, but I wasn't given a lot of choice. It wasn't a, "You are invited to . . ." it was more, "You are expected to . . ." The big treat was "hot dogs." I hadn't seen a hot dog in almost a year. The Ambassador was having hot dogs flown in for his Fourth of July picnic.

As I pulled the VW into the driveway of the Ambassador's mansion, I was struck by the opulence that surrounded me. The house was a large, stately building surrounded by manicured lawns, decorative trees, and lush flower beds. There were uniformed attendants parking the guests' cars, and uniformed servants greeting and announcing visitors.

A parking attendant said he would park my car and told me to go up the steps to the door where I was met by an African man who checked a list for my name. He then called an African woman in a black dress with a white apron and cap. She escorted me through the mansion to the back door which opened on to a lawn. There were several Americans there already. The backyard contained a large red and white awning which was erected over several tables. There were people standing in groups and sitting at the tables talking and laughing. Children were playing croquet and volleyball. There were men throwing horseshoes and people swimming in the pool. The servants were going through the crowd carrying serving trays of hors d'oeuvres and wine. There was a bar set up under the awning where bottles of Budweiser beer were nestled in ice waiting to quench the thirst of patriotic Americans celebrating the Fourth of July. Only one thing was missing—the hot dogs! What's Fourth of July without a hot dog? We had been told that the Ambassador would be serving American hot dogs. WHERE ARE THE HOT DOGS?

"Ladies and Gentlemen." It was Ambassador Stebbins on the loudspeaker. "We had hot dogs flown into the country for this celebration. However, the Ugandan Government held up the shipment for inspection. The hot dogs sat in the airport warehouse for several days awaiting government import inspection. By the time they were released to us, they were spoiled. I am sorry, but we will have to substitute English sausages." "OHHH, What a place." People are expressing their disappointment. "So, what do you expect? It's typical of Uganda." It seemed ironic to me that the commemoration of American independence from England, would have to be celebrated with English sausages.

Who was Ambassador Henry Endicott Stebbins? *Who's Who in America* tells us about his background. He was born in Milton, Massachusetts, the son of Roderick and Edith Endicott. He received the AB degree from Harvard University. Twenty-four years after graduating from Harvard, he married Barbara Worthington. He was a "career" diplomat and worked in American Embassies in Switzerland, Istanbul, London, Canada, Vienna, Paris, Australia, Nepal, India, and, finally, Uganda.

He was an interesting person to talk to. I had the opportunity of talking with Ambassador Stebbins that Fourth of July day. He was telling me about his days prior to World War II when he was working with Ambassador

Joseph Kennedy in the American Embassy in London. I told him that I had heard that Ambassador Kennedy had advised President Roosevelt against entering WWII. He hedged on this, saying that there were a lot of Americans who didn't want to go to war. They felt it was a "European War" and that the United States should stay out of. They were opposed to sending American boys to die in Europe. Ambassador Stebbins made me feel that this wasn't a subject which he cared to discuss. He thanked me for attending the picnic and drifted off through the crowd.

An even more interesting question than "Who was Henry Endicott Stebbins?" is the question, "What ever happened to Henry Endicott Stebbins?" The closest answer to that question comes from an article in the *New York Times,* dated March 29, 1973:

RETIRED U.S. ENVOY IS REPORTED MISSING FROM A LINER AT SEA

Henry Endicott Stebbins, a retired American diplomat from Milton, Mass., was reported missing at sea and presumed dead today after the Italian liner *Leonardo da Vinci* docked in Lisbon.

Mr. Stebbins, 67 years old, was Ambassador to Nepal from 1959 to 1966 and Ambassador to Uganda from 1966 to 1969, when he retired.

The Captain of the liner, Claudio Cosulich, told the authorities that Mr. Stebbins was last seen early Wednesday when his wife, Barbara, left him on deck to go to her cabin. Mrs. Stebbins had a separate cabin and did not realize that her husband was missing until just before lunch Wednesday.

His watch and other valuables were spread on the

dressing table, but he apparently had not undressed. The bed had not been occupied.

Mrs. Stebbins promptly reported his absence to the ship's officers, who conducted a search of the 22,000-ton liner. They concluded that he had fallen overboard at a time when the sea was rough.

At the time that Mr. Stebbin's disappearance was confirmed. the ship was 300 miles from its midnight location, and the captain judged it useless to turn back.

The ship's arrival in Lisbon was a day late because of bad weather.

The American consul in Lisbon, Donald B. Wallace, went to the ship to investigate the disappearance.

American Embassy sources said that Mr. Stebbins and his wife boarded the ship in New York last week, bound for a vacation in Italy.

The question remains, "What Ever Happened to Henry Endicott Stebbins?" I have been told that there was more to this story than has been told, and that there might have been "money" involved in the Stebbins disappearance. But, I leave that to others to investigate.

22

I had given up my R&R, but I hadn't given up the idea of spending my summer vacation in Europe. Joyce and the children had not taken the direct flight back to the States. They had flown from Entebbe to London, and then from London to New York. If I could find a "cheap" round-trip from Entebbe to London and return, I could meet my family in London for a European summer.

The travel agent in Tororo was Didi Bawa. If anyone could get me to London and back for a low price, it was Didi Bawa. After all, his "religion" had gotten people to the moon, and it hadn't cost as much as it did for American astronauts to go there. When I was building my Swahili vocabulary, I asked Patel at Tororo General, "What's the Swahili word for cheap?" To which Patel answered, "Didi Bawa."

Didi Bawa's travel agency was just up and across the street from Patel's Tororo General where we did our grocery shopping. I had often seen Didi sitting under the awning in front of his shop. He was a huge man. I would guess he weighed almost 300 pounds. He always wore a white shirt and tie as he sat beside a small, round table drinking tea and reading a newspaper.

I parked my car in front of Tororo General and crossed the street to Didi's shop. He was sitting next to the shop door drinking tea, as usual. "Good morning, Mr. Bawa," I said as I approached his shop. "Oh, good morning to you, sir. May I pour you a cup of tea?" He said, as he offered a seat to me. As we drank tea together, I explained that I was looking for an affordable round-trip flight to London. Didi got up from his chair, and I followed him into his office. His desk and chair were piled high with papers. He rummaged through the papers and extracted a single sheet from the pile. "This is a fine charter flight that is the very thing that you want." He said.

Didi Bawa was able to get me on a charter flight from Entebbe to London and return for $500. The TWA charter was going to leave Entebbe on August 1 and would return September 2. This would give me a month in Europe with Joyce and the kids. Great! I wrote to Joyce telling her that I would be in London August 1 and would meet her and the children at Heathrow Airport. Joyce would take a flight to London as soon after August 1 as she could. We would then spend the summer touring Europe. I would return on my charter flight September 2, and she would follow on her flight with the kids.

Didi Bawa's charter flight was filled with Asians who were visiting relatives in the UK. Asian families were being "encouraged" to leave East Africa by black African governments. The days were numbered for Asians in Uganda. Soon they would be forced out of East Africa and would have to move to England.

Idi Amin overthrew Milton Obote in January of 1971. One year later, in August of 1972, he ordered all Asians out of Uganda. Their homes, and businesses, as well as everything else they owned was taken by the Uganda Government. Then they were loaded on air planes with only a change of clothing and "dumped" in Britain.

The New York Times had the following article, dated August 19,

UGANDA SAYS THAT ALL ASIANS, EVEN CITIZENS, MUST LEAVE COUNTRY

KAMPALA, Uganda. Aug. 19—President Idi Amin in a surprise move, announced today that all Asians in Uganda—even citizens—would be expelled.

"This will be carried out as a second-phase operation after the present one involving the Asians holding British passports and nationals of India, Pakistan and Bangladesh," President Amin said in the town of Rukungiri.

Early this month, President Amin announced that all Asians holding or entitled to British passports must leave with 90 days because they were "economic saboteurs."

Most of the Asians in Uganda are Indians and Pakistanis whose parents came here at the turn of the century to open small shops and work as businessmen. Since then, the Asian community has prospered and is believed to control as much as 90 percent of Uganda's commerce and trade. . . .

The announcement means that virtually the entire Asian community will disappear, leaving businesses, schools, stores, banks, garages, hospitals, and hotels in the hands of Ugandans for the first time.

The charter flight Didi Bawa had gotten me on was filled with Asian women in saris with their children. It wasn't a good trip to London. Every seat on the plane was filled. It would have been impossible to squeeze even one more person into the plane. Asian women were holding young children on their laps, so that some seats had double occupancy. Some of the women were getting airsick, and the stewardesses were running about the cabin cleaning up one mess after another. It was a long, unpleasant trip. I heard one of the American TWA stewardesses say, "I'LL NEVER work one of these Asian charter flights again!" I didn't blame her. I still had the return to look forward to.

I got out of the plane at London's Heathrow and stepped back into the modern world. I collected my luggage and started through the terminal, when I saw a drinking fountain. I had to stop and drink water from that drinking fountain. Water right from the tap! No boiling, no filtering—just clear, fresh, delicious water. It was a treat for me to do this. Just like grandma said, "What will they think of next?" The water from that fountain was so good, I stopped at the next drinking fountain and had one more.

Now, let's see; how do I get to Victoria Station from the airport? I thought. There were a lot of black, English taxis in front of the airport terminal waiting to pick up passengers. I spoke to a man outside the terminal and asked, "How do I get to Victoria Station from here?" "Well, Gov'ner, you'll take one of these taxis. I'm free now and can take you meself." "How much is that going to be?" I asked. "It'll be 20 pounds, standard rate." "Twenty pounds, let's see," I thought. "That's going to be over thirty dollars!" "Twenty pounds!" I said. "I didn't think it would be that expensive." "That's what it is, lad." "You won't get in to Victoria any cheaper, and you won't get there any faster. You can take my word for that," he said. Just then, an English policeman came along and asked if I needed any assistance. "How am I going to get in to Victoria Station?" I asked. "Just go down to the middle of the building where those people are queued up for the BOAC bus. It will drop you off at Victoria." He said. "Do you know the price?" I asked. "The fare is two pounds." He replied. I looked at the taxi driver, and he just smiled, shrugged his shoulders, and walked away. I wonder how many tourists pay the 20 pounds and take the taxi? A variation of this same thing has happened every time I have been at London's Heathrow.

I had a paperback entitled *Europe on $5 a Day*. I think that this publication must have raised its rates per day by now. The book listed a hotel that catered to families. It was described as inexpensive, clean, and centrally located at 68 Belgrave Road near Victoria Station. It is recommended by the author who said it's owned by some people from Spain. So, off I went in search of the Hansel and Gretel Hotel. I found the Hansel and Gretel and rented a large room with five beds—one double and four singles. Now, I was all ready for the family to arrive. I went down the hall, took a bath—there was not a bath in the room, just one bath on the floor—came back to the room, and went to sleep. It had been a long trip.

The next day, I rolled over, looked at my watch, and sat up. I had been sleeping over ten hours. There was a lot to do. I still had to find transportation. One of the British teachers at Manjasi Boys School in Tororo had told me I could rent a "caravan" from Steven's Garage on High Street. I called the number I had been given, and a man said, "Hello, Steven's Garage." "Hello," I replied, "I live in Tororo, Uganda, East Africa. Bernard Crix gave me your name and telephone number and said that I might be able to rent a caravan from you for the month of August. I have a wife and four small children. We would like to spend the month traveling on the Continent." "Bernard Crix," he said? "You know Bernard Crix? How is old Bernard? I haven't seen him in years." He sounded excited to meet a "Yank" that knew Bernard from Uganda. He asked about Bernard, Uganda, and just what I needed in a vehicle for the month of August. At the end of the conversation, I had secured a "Bluebird Highwayman" caravan that would sleep four children and two adults, had a toilet, and a kitchen. It would be ideal for us. I had accomplished a lot during my first day in London.

Joyce and the children arrived about 9 a.m. the next morning. I was getting to know my way around the Victoria Station section of London pretty well. I also knew how to get to and from Victoria Station. I took the B.O.A.C. bus to the airport and waited for the family to arrive. When I saw them, they looked like I had "felt" when I got off the plane from Entebbe. They had gotten on the plane about 11 p.m. in New York. It was now 9 a.m. in England, and they hadn't slept well during the flight.

After getting the luggage and passing through customs, we ended up at the same point I had been a couple of days before. There were the taxis and the offers of the 20-pound ride into Victoria Station. "No, thanks, Gov'ner," I said, "We'll take the B.O.A.C. bus."

I wanted to show everyone what I had discovered walking around Victoria Station, but Joyce and the kids just wanted to go to bed. So, they went to sleep, while I read the *New York Times* I had purchased at Heathrow.

We transferred our luggage to the caravan at Steven's Garage and headed for the coast and the ferry to France. It was good to see the kids again. They were full of stories about America and their friends. They asked about the Gatchells, Williams, and Tororo Girls School. I told them about our new house and neighbors. "I'm going to miss the Gatchells and the Williams children." Stephen said. "Maybe there will be new families with children your age," I told Stephen.

Driving in England was easier for me than I had expected. We had been driving on the "English" side of the road for the last year in Uganda. We drove to Dover and boarded the ferry. It was a much bigger boat than I had imagined. I drove the caravan down into the ship's lower deck, which looked like a parking lot the size of a football field. After we parked the caravan, we went up on deck. It was raining—it always rains in Britain—so we stayed in the lounge during the entire trip. The rain was coming down so hard we couldn't see out of the windows very well. There wasn't much to see anyway. Just ocean and grey clouds. The channel crossing seemed to take forever. There wasn't a lot to do, especially for the children. As always, they had books and toys to play with. The girls had dolls, and the boys had matchbook trucks and cars. I was thankful that the children were all still tired from their flight through five time zones and slept most of the way.

When we drove the caravan off the boat in France, the weather had changed and was sunny. What an adventure it was going to be—a summer in Europe! As we drove up the French coast the ocean beach was on our left and the beautiful countryside of France was on our right. I had never imagined that I would ever be able to take a vacation like this with my family. I looked over at Joyce, who seemed deep in thought, and said, "What are you thinking about?" "I was just wishing that this were the road between Alfred and Vestal and that we would be visiting our parents soon." Joyce said. "Is that what you are thinking?" She asked. "The road between Alfred and Vestal?" I said. "That's the farthest thing from my mind. I was enjoying the thought that we are on our way to Belgium, Holland, Germany, Italy, and Switzerland. We've just finished a nice seafood dinner on the coast of the English Channel and are about to spend a summer in Europe!" Joyce was homesick. We had never traveled before, and I didn't realize that she hated being away from home and family. I thought back to the time when I had read the advertisement in the *New York Times,* "Teach Business Subjects in East Africa," and had asked Joyce, "How would you like to go to Africa?" She had replied, "I am happy just where I am. You go, I'll stay here with the children." Now, a year later, I could see that she really didn't like to travel. Africa and Europe were not as "exciting" to her as they were to me. I just couldn't understand how she could not enjoy travel. I loved every minute of it. It was going to be a long year for Joyce. She was less than half way through this "adventure."

Steven's Garage had given us a map of the campsites in Europe. Camping is very popular among Europeans, and some of the campsites are like little villages. They have all the accommodations one might require. There are hot showers, laundry facilities, swimming pools, playgrounds, restaurants, supermarkets, pharmacies, beauty salons for the women, and barbershops for the men. Some campsites are located on the ocean and have beaches for swimming, complete with lifeguards. Our map listed the facilities each campsite had. We choose one of these campsites and pulled in for the night.

The children worked off some energy on the playground, while Joyce did some grocery shopping, and fixed dinner in the caravan's kitchen. By the time it was dark, we were all ready for a good night's sleep. There was a small bed over the front seats for John. The sofa became a double bed, bunks pulled down from the ceiling, and there was a double bed in the rear of the vehicle. Just enough room for the six of us. I went to sleep dreaming of tomorrow's "adventure." I think Joyce must have gone to sleep dreaming of the road between Alfred and Vestal.

23

The next morning we got up, had breakfast in the caravan, and set off for Belgium. Traveling with four small children through Europe is something that I wouldn't recommend. In Belgium we stopped and took a tour of some castle. The kids weren't interested in the castle. We had passed a carnival on the way to the castle. The kids wanted to ride the Ferris wheel. I wanted to "see" Europe. I didn't want to ride a Ferris wheel.

We went on to Amsterdam and took a boat ride through the canals of the city. The kids liked the boat ride, but wanted to play in the water. "John! Get away from the water. Can't you see that it's dirty? Don't get your shoes wet. John!" It was a continual "Don't do this. Don't do that."

From Holland we drove through Germany, finally ending up in Bavaria—King Ludwig's castles. "John, don't throw your apple in the pool. That's the king's pool. What will the king say when he sees your half-eaten apple floating in his pool?" I had to take off my shoes and socks and wade in the king's pool to retrieve John's apple core.

Ever try to find mustard in a German supermarket? The labels are all in a "foreign" language. Don't these people speak English? Try the pharmacy—I want to find mouthwash. Listerine. Lister was a German, wasn't he? "Listerine—Lister. Mouthwash. AHHHHH." I opened my mouth and went through the act of mouth washing. "OHH! Yah." They understood.

We were on the beach in Italy. A beautiful campsite on the Italian Mediterranean. "Where's John? John is gone!" There were thousands of people on the beach, and we lost John. I approached a policeman and showed him John's passport picture. I couldn't speak Italian, but I knew the German word "kinder" "Dar kinder is louse!" The policeman knew what I meant—John is missing. Where is John? Thousands of people. Somewhere in that crowd was a child who answered to the name, "John." Where? After a two-hour search we found John. He had been found by someone and turned in to the campsite office, just like a lost umbrella. He was crying. "John!" We gave him big hugs and kisses. Everybody was smiling. We need a leash for this kid! "John, you stay by Daddy. Don't wander off by yourself."

We drove through Switzerland. I stopped at a campsite and registered. A colleague from State University of New York told me to sign "Professor" and I would be given special treatment while I was in Europe. "The Europeans have great respect for educators," he said. So, I signed the book "Professor William D. Stewart." The woman at the desk looked at the signature and spoke to me in German. I replied "Non-spragen Deutch." The woman spoke to me in French. I shook my head. I didn't even know the French words meaning, "I don't speak French." The woman spoke to me in Italian. I shook my head again—no Italian. Then the woman spoke to me in English. "You don't speak French. You don't speak German. You don't speak Italian, and you call yourself 'professor'?" What kind of 'professor' are you?" Boy! Did I feel "stupid" or what? I never signed "Professor William D. Stewart" again.

We were in Northern Italy. There were no campsites

here. It was a small town. We were in a grocery store buying "fixins" for the evening meal in the caravan. What to drink? The store was very small. There was no milk for the children's dinner. There were no soft drinks. There was wine. "Do you give this to children?" I asked. The wine was in an unlabeled, light-green bottle (liter size) with a wire contraption that held a rubber stopper. The woman assured me that this was a table wine which was suitable for "family drinking." We bought the wine and had it with the evening meal. It tasted a little like apple cider. That night all four children wet the bed. Great stuff!

In Venice we had lunch in a small cafe on St. Mark's Square. The kids had to "check out" the bathroom. This was a favorite thing. "I have to go to the bathroom," were the first words that John and Stephen ever spoke. There was the bathroom door. Stephen wanted to be first. He tried the door. It was locked. Someone was using the bathroom. He waited next to the door. After a while, the door opened and out stepped a woman. The bathroom was coed. Stephen stepped through the door and closed it behind him. We were all waiting the first reports on the bathroom. Stephen opened the door and staggered out. "Dad! You gotta see this bathroom." John had to go the bathroom. He needed assistance, so I took his hand and entered the door. YUUKK!! Now I knew what Stephen meant. The bathroom was an empty room. It had a cement floor with an incline that went down to a "ditch" in the center. On the floor are piles of "Poops." You pick a spot, drop your pants, squat, and "do your duty" on the cement floor. Every once in a while, someone must wash the "duties" down to the ditch in the center of the room. Amazing. "John, take your pants down and do "poo-poo" on the floor," I said. John was not having any part of this and headed for the door. When we returned to the table, everyone was interested to find out what was behind that door.

"Joyce," I said, "You've got to see that bathroom. Take the girls in and check that out. Paula and Beth wanted to take a look. What's behind that door? They went through the door and came right back out. "Oh! Dad, that stinks!" Beth said. We all just shook our head and laughed. Now, that's a bathroom!

The rest areas on the Italian highways are "different" also. The men stand along one side of the building and "do a number one" on a tile wall. Number two's are done inside. I only had to do a number one. John liked this arrangement. Stephen was a little shy. He stood so close to the tiles, I thought he would fall in. He just didn't want anyone to see him. The girls and mother went around the other side of the building and through the door. Women do both "one's and "two's" inside.

We had seen enough of the Continent. It wasn't fun with the children. They were too young to enjoy what we were doing. However, they did like the Leaning Tower of Pisa and the Eiffel Tower in Paris. There were also the boat rides in Amsterdam and Paris. The rest was boring to them. So, back to "Jolly old" England we went. From England we drove up to Scotland. In Edinburgh we saw a lot of people standing in line on the main street. So, we got in line. "What's this line for," I asked. "It for tickets to the Tattoo." A man answered. "What's the Tattoo?" I replied. He went on to explain that it was an annual performance given at the castle. There would be bagpipers, acrobats, and a demonstration by the Scottish Army. It sounded good, so we stayed in line and got tickets. The kids liked the Tattoo. It was much like a circus.

The month was about over, and we had to go back to

Uganda. It seemed strange to think of going "home" to Africa. The entire year had been like a vacation. We drove back to London, returned the caravan to Steven's Garage, and checked into a hotel. This time we stayed in a bigger hotel that had shuttle service to the airport. I would be leaving a day before Joyce and the kids and would meet them at the airport in Entebbe. The morning I left England, I remember the soft-boiled eggs I had for breakfast. The egg shells had a little "crown" stamped on one end. The next day I would be at home in Tororo looking at eggs covered with chicken manure.

I said "goodbye" to Joyce and the kids, got on my "charter" flight with the Asians, and started thinking, "What are you going back to Africa for?" I was getting homesick all over again.

24

I arrived in Uganda a day before the family and had gotten a room at the Apollo Hotel instead of at The Grand, where we usually stayed. The Apollo Hotel, which was under construction during our first year in Uganda, was now completed. The hotel was a little away from the center of Kampala's downtown activity, but the modern rooms with a balcony overlooking the city made up for it. It was a nice change from The Grand. The price was a bit higher than The Grand, but what the heck, we could "splurge" a little just this once.

I thought everyone would be tired after the airplane trip from London, and they were. It was nice not to have to look forward to the drive to Tororo right after the flight. It was getting toward evening, so we drove right to the Apollo and went to bed.

At breakfast the next morning, I tried some of the Apollo's "Kippered Herring." I had never had fish for breakfast before. The kids all said "YUUKK!," but it tasted good to me. After one last "stroll" through the tourist section of Kampala, we drove back to Tororo. No DIVERSION this time, and we were in Tororo in time to have lunch at The Rock Hotel.

Instead of turning right to go to our old house on the TGS campus, I turned left and drove to our new house in Tororo. Everyone liked the new quarters much better. The kids walked through all the rooms; "Which is my room?" "Which is my bed?" "Where do I sleep?" The kids were all talking at once. They inspected the bedrooms, the kitchen, and the bathroom. "Hey, Dad," Stephen said, "The bananas on our tree are growing upside down." "Dad," said Paula, "We've got oranges on our tree." "Look, John," Beth said, "There's our school. That's where you're going to go to school. Right next to our back yard." Beth and Paula took John through the backyard to look at the school. Everyone was happy with our new living conditions.

There was one thing, however, that I had not considered with the move off campus. Thieves! The houses on the TGS campus didn't have a problem with thieves. The campus and surrounding area was well lit, and the school had guards on duty at night. Our new house had none of these advantages. There were no streetlights. There were no fences between houses. Perfect conditions for evening thieves. Our neighbors, the Richters, had a big Alsatian—Simba. "Simba" is the Swahili word for "lion." Simba was a lion of a dog. The Richters did not have a "thief" problem with Simba around. We had less than a year left—so who's counting?—however, and a dog was not practical for us.

One evening, while reading, I heard a "clink." Someone had dropped a galvanized pipe in our attached garage. Someone's in our garage! I thought. We have a lot of "stuff" in the garage. "Stuff" that thieves take—bicycles, the Vespa, tools, etc. What to do? "Joyce," I whispered. "Someone is in the garage. I am going to go down to Richter's and bring Simba back with me. When I go out the front door, lock it and stay inside." I slipped through the front door, and Joyce locked it behind me. I walked through the front yard to the Richters. When I knocked on the door, Simba came growling and barking to the door.

"Good boy, Simba. We're going to chase some thieves tonight. Good boy." I knocked on the door again. Then, I realized that the Richters were not home. Here I was, standing alone in the African night with thieves in my garage. Not a good place to be. What was I going to do? I had to get back to the safety of my house. So, back across the front yard to my door I went, scuffing my feet to keep the snakes out of the way, saying "Good boy, Simba. Get 'em, Simba. Get 'em! Good boy, Simba. Good boy!" I tapped on our front door and whispered, "Joyce! Let me in, quick!" When I got behind the safety of the locked door; Joyce said, "When you were down to Richter's, five men jumped off the roof and ran through the back yard." They were on the roof while I was walking alone, unarmed in the yard below.

That was enough of that. I decided to hire an evening guard. The Swahili word is "Eskari" for these guards. This eskari sits outside your door at night. You must supply the eskari with a woolen blanket and a "panga" (a bush knife about two foot long.) As I drove down the street at night, I could see these eskaris sitting on front porches, wrapped in these blankets with panga in hand.

Thieving is common in Uganda. It seemed that everyone was stealing from us. We had a problem with Francis stealing. We were losing a lot from the kitchen. One Sunday, we counted all the silverware, cups, plates, and glasses in the kitchen. We recounted the following Sunday and were surprised at just how much was disappearing from the kitchen. The following Monday morning, I went out to see Francis in the servant's quarters. I told him I thought he was stealing from us and made a search of his room. There were all of the missing items plus much more from the children's rooms. He had our coffee, tea, soap, flour, sugar, clothing, vitamin pills, razors, soap, aftershave. The list went on and on. I am sure there was much more that he had sold to others in town. "Oh!" said the girls, "there's my doll!" This was too much. It's hard to believe that the house servant who has complete freedom in your home is stealing.

I thought we were treating Francis well. He was making more than he would have been paid if he worked for other "Europeans." Then, too, what about the time his wife was sick? He came to me one day saying that he had brought his wife in from the village because she was sick. Francis stayed in the servant's quarters during the week. On the weekends he went back to his home in the village and his wife. One Monday he brought his wife back from the village with him. He said she was sick. I took Francis and his wife to one of the English doctors in Tororo. The doctor made his diagnosis—gonorrhea! Francis didn't know what that was or what that meant. We paid the doctor for the woman's treatment.

We couldn't live with a thief, so I had to let Francis go. Francis asked if I would write a letter of recommendation for him. I wrote the following:

TO WHOM IT MAY CONCERN

This is to introduce Francis to you. He has been our house servant for a year. During that time, he has been cleaning our house out for us.

Should you hire him, I am sure that he will clean your house out also. He cleans out so well, you will not have anything left.
Sincerely,
William D. Stewart

Francis was happy with the letter. He couldn't read

English, but he was sure this would help him get another job.

From that time on, we did without a house servant. The new house had wooden floors and would not require the waxing that the cement floors in the TGS houses did. We also had a washing machine in the new house. So, Joyce would be able to handle the household work. One British couple told me that after 15 years of living in Africa they had never had a houseboy who wasn't a thief.

We also had to get a new "eskari" (evening guard). Our eskari asked me for another woolen blanket and panga. He said that thieves had stolen his while he was sleeping one evening. Great protection!

Thieving was not any better in Kenya. We took a week's vacation in Mombasa. Beachcomber Cottages had been recommended to us. These cottages were part of a resort complex on the Indian Ocean. There was a main hotel with a pool and six cottages for families along the beach. One morning I found that my swimming trunks had been stolen from the clothes line. So much had been stolen from me that, when I saw an African walking along the beach in front of the cottage with my trunks on, I decided I would get these back. I wrote the following letter to a Bill Gatchell about this episode.

> Dear Bill:
>
> The last "Uganda Report" went out with all the enthusiasm and cheer of one who was about to enjoy the pleasures of Beachcomber Cottages near Mombasa on the Indian Ocean. I must admit, however, that the next few days turned our dreams into a nightmare.
>
> As the sun rose on Pismo Beach (I refer to Beachcomber as such) we decided to take a swim in the only available place—the pool at the Windblown Hotel next door. I say "only available," as we had long since

abandoned the north beach of Mombasa to the creeping and crawling things that peered out from the slimy, dirty weeds.

Ah yes! The next morning. We start for the pool; but, "Alas!" My bathing suit is astray! Where can it be? The watchman (trusted and true) insists that I must have mislaid it—simple minded man that I am. But, Ah, no! What is this? A young, dark-skinned lad with a familiar pair of trunks strolling the beach in front of my humble abode.

"Good morning," said I. "Jumbo," said he. "Yes, they are a bit big on you, but I believe that the label says "large," not "jumbo." That is, my dear fellow," I continued, "I believe you adorn yourself with my apparel."

The poor man was visibly shaken, but unmoved in his explanation that the shorts were the gracious gift of a former visitor at the hotel. What to do? Other vacationers on the beach advise a visit to the manager of the hotel who will be able to verify the gentleman's story and diagnose that I am the victim of sunstroke.

The arrangements are made. We stroll arm and arm down the beach to the manager. We near the manager's cottage on the edge of the jungle when my steadfast friend remembers an important engagement in some far distant village. Important man that he is, he finds it impossible to advise me of his plans, and bounds with the utmost of enthusiasm into the bush. Thus, leaving me to make my way to the manager alone. After waiting for a reasonable period of time, the manager and I conclude that my friend has betrayed my confidence.

Even though confidence has been betrayed, justice will reign! The police shall be sought. ("Sought" being the proper word, as the local authorities have no other transportation than the unreliable bus system.) Three hours later, after all the proper forms, statements, and claims are in order, we start on our search. Cleaver fellows, these East African detectives. Scotland Yard would be put to shame by their plan of attack—a four-hour hunt through the bush during the hottest part of the tropical day, when the thief is sure to be resting from the sweltering sun.

The hours go by. We trek through bush, bush, and more bush. Finally, we find ourselves on the main road, where the detectives conclude that we have been alluded by our wily adversary. "Bloody scoundrel!" (As the English say.) But sorrow not for my blistered feet, or my sunburned body and scratched legs. Sorrow for the poor wretch that even now has to roam that lonely beach in those oversized drawers.

Having had a taste of the "local color," we concluded that our stay at Beachcomber should be terminated the following morning. Plans were made and bags were packed; but, unthoughtful of details in our attempt to flee, a child's case containing 20 shillings was left within six feet of an open, though barred, window. How could we be so cruel as to place temptation before such weak vessels?

In the still of the tropical night, a long, thin stick glides silently through the bars of the window, coming to rest under the handle of the case. Just as silently, the stick and case glide back through the bars. The deed is done with only the morning light to disclose what has taken place. Of the distress, tears, woe, and tumult I shall not here comment; but, rather leave this to your imagination.

The trip back reaches its perfect conclusion, as I arrive home to discover that I have a temperature of 102 degrees. A search for a doctor, a quick examination, and all is revealed. I have malaria and spend the next six days in bed.

How did the folder read? Something about a wonderful time in Mombasa? I can't quite remember. One thing I am sure of, however, is that I agree with that bird watcher of old who said: A pair of trunks in the hand is worth two in the bush." (or something like that.) Bwana Bill Stewart

This letter expresses how we were feeling at this time. It seemed that someone was always stealing something from us. I was just "sick of it" and wanted to get my swimming trunks back. But, not only was this a waste of time; I got malaria going through the jungle. Sometimes, you just can't win.

I can also see "the other side of the coin." We had so much more than the African people around us. What was a pair of trunks, or a few pieces of silverware to us?

25

The man who was replacing Don Williams arrived in Tororo with his wife and family. Paul and Dodie Mott were from Colorado. They had two young girls about the same ages as Beth and Paula. It's too bad we lived in Tororo Town now. Our girls would not be as close to the Mott children as they were with the Gatchell's young ones.

Paul had worked with Phyllis Roop in the Denver area as the principal of one of the schools there. I imagine that Phyllis had "talked" Paul into coming to TGS. He was an able administrator—very "sharp."

The Motts moved into the house that Don and Jackie Williams had occupied. It was a smooth transition. Paul worked well with Phyllis. He didn't seem to be going through the "culture shock" that I had experienced. Nor did he seem to require the "help" that I had needed from Gatchell, Williams, and Andrezejewski. I guess the Motts were getting whatever support they needed from Phyllis. The Motts were not as close to us as the Gatchells or Andrezejewskis. Perhaps it was because we now lived in town and were not living next door. At any rate, we didn't seem to have a lot in common. He didn't "think" the way I did about things. Paul was a "by the book" kind of guy with a "chapter and verse" approach for what he did. I sort of "flew by the seat of my pants" taking each problem that came up as "unique" without a textbook approach.

For example, we took gamma globulin shots every six months. The GG was given to us via the Embassy/Peace Corps. It was for the American personnel at TGS. Since my wife was a nurse, we had the GG in our refrigerator. American faculty and staff came to our house for GG shots every six months. We had so much GG, that it would reach the "Expiration Date" and be thrown away. We threw a lot of it away. It just got too old to use. As far as I know, the American Embassy was the only source of GG in Uganda. It couldn't be purchased anywhere.

We knew a British couple in Tororo. The husband had a doctorate in one of the sciences and was working for a local industry. His wife had a degree in the arts and had taught some English courses for us at TGS on a part-time basis. One day this man showed up at our door and asked if we could give his wife and him an injection of GG. She had come down with hepatitis, and they were scared. A British doctor had sent them to us as the only source of what he had prescribed—GG. "Of course," we said, and Joyce gave them the amount the British doctor had suggested.

The next day, Paul Mott wanted to talk with me. He said, "You are going to be asked to provide GG for a local British couple. That GG is for Americans only. I don't want you to give these British the GG." Now, I was in trouble. We had already done the "dirty deed." "Paul," I said, "We have so much of this GG that we are just throwing it away as it expires. You know that these people need this GG and can't get it anyplace else. I think we should, under these circumstances, give them the medication they need." Paul raised his voice a bit and insisted that I not, under any circumstances, give this GG to anyone but Americans.

Well, it was already done. Too bad, Paul. Not only are

you "dead wrong" on this one; you are a day late as well. So, I told the British couple what Paul had said and asked that they not tell anyone about it. Even if we had not already given the shots, I would have done it anyway. I could sleep better at night knowing I had broken an Embassy rule than knowing I had refused to help relieve a person's pain, suffering, or death. What is that "bullshit?" That's American Embassy/USAID stuff. Will Muller tried to pull that crap on us when my wife needed to go to the States for surgery.

The same kind of thing happened at the end of our tour. We had end-of-tour contract provision for 500 pounds of airfreight to the States for each person in the family. Since there were six of us, that meant we could take 3,000 pounds of airfreight back to the States with us. We would never send that much airfreight back.

There was a Peace Corps couple from Oklahoma who had been assigned to TGS. Henry and Lucille Simmons had both retired from teaching. They were in their 60s; but instead of retiring, they joined the Peace Corps and were assigned to TGS. USAID owed them a lot. They were both filling TGS positions on Peace Corps salary with benefits that were nothing compared to what USAID people received. Their Peace Corps contract did not allow airfreight back to the States. They came by our house with a three foot by three foot cardboard box and asked if we had room in our return freight for it. It couldn't have weighed more than 30 pounds. We had at least 1,000 pounds that we were not using, so we shipped it off with ours. When we got to the States, we sent it on to their Oklahoma address. Along comes Paul Mott with a warning not to ship anything for Henry and Lucille Simmons. Apparently, they had asked his permission. So, sue me. I sent it. Paul should have been happy to do anything he could for these two Peace Corps people. TGS was getting their services practically free of charge.

Those are some examples that prove that I would never be a good administrator. Some administrators don't "think" or "question." Some administrators don't "care" about people. These are the blind-faith "doers" of the word. USAID is filled with these kind of people.

The teachers at TGS were free of this kind of pressure. It's hard to try to "force" people to do something if there isn't an incentive. The proverbial "carrot" in front of the horse. What's USAID, the Embassy, U. Mass, or Paul Mott going to do to me if I follow my conscience and do what's contrary to what they want? Fire me? Refuse to renew my contract? Deny a pay increase? Tell my mother? There was nothing they could do to me. I did as I thought best, whether Paul Mott, USAID, U. Mass, or the Embassy liked it or not. I was absolutely free. It was wonderful!

The semester went on as the others had. We taught classes, went to The Club swimming with the kids, did our shopping at Tororo General and the open-air market, and wrote letters home—lots of letters home.

I played chess with George Andrezejewski, read my *Newsweek* magazine, listened to the BBC and The Voice of America (in special English). Life was not quite the same at TGS without the Gatchells. Our kids missed their kids, and I missed Bill and Ellen. No one else at TGS had the answers to all of the world's problems like Bill did. He was a real "philosopher," and I missed our discussions.

We didn't have many centipedes at the house in town. Even if I brought centipedes home from TGS, the children couldn't have played "centipede hockey" at our new home. We had cement blocks on the porch with ridges between the blocks and the "centipede pucks" wouldn't slide very far.

Stephen and Paula were doing well with their Calvert courses. Joyce spent about three hours a day with them. That's all it took to keep up with their grade level in the States. There are no distractions or discipline problems with home teaching. No one talks back to the teacher, whispers, giggles, passes notes, shows up without having done homework, has to go to gym, the office, the nurse, or the principal. Everyone pays attention, listens to the teacher, and does the homework—ideal! Three hours a day, and they were able to keep up. Does that tell you something about American classrooms?

John and Beth were busy in the Asian school. Every morning they went out the backdoor and walked across our backyard to the school. They came home for lunch every day. John was starting to pick up a bit of an English accent. If he didn't like something, he said it was "a lot of roobish." He also liked "crisps," "sweets," and "squash."

There were some places that we wanted to visit before we left Uganda. It seemed that we had just arrived and gotten settled in our Tororo Town house. Now, we would soon be giving it up. I was going to miss Tororo, but I had to return or lose my position at SUNY. Sometimes I couldn't wait to return to the States, and other times I hated the thought of giving up the "good life" in Uganda.

We had been to Nairobi, Mombasa, England, France, Belgium, Holland, Germany, Italy, and Switzerland. However, before we left East Africa, we wanted to see Mount Kilimanjaro, ride down the Nile River at Murchison Falls, and visit Treetops.

Mount Kilimanjaro and Treetops would be one trip. These lodges are both in Kenya. Treetops is an hour's drive north of Nairobi, and Mount Kilimanjaro is a couple of hours south of Nairobi. We made reservations for our Christmas vacation.

This was going to be our last trip to Nairobi—back down the road to Eldoret, past the "ELEPHANTS HAVE THE RIGHT OF WAY and EAT WELL AT THE BELL signs, Lake Nakuru and the flamingos, up the escarpment, past the African basket makers, and into The Fair View. We had been to Nairobi several times during the past year, and what had been "spectacular" to us, had become "everyday." We didn't photograph the flamingos, the elephants, or the giraffe. We didn't stop to see the African basket makers, or go to Bazaar Street. We just drove to The Fair View, had dinner, and went to bed. We had not been to Treetops, and we were looking forward to that.

After a leisurely breakfast, we drove north from Nairobi, through Fort Hall, and to Treetops. Treetops is just what it sounds like—a game lodge in the top of trees. The lodge is too big to be entirely supported by trees. There are trees growing up through the buildings, but these buildings are supported by traditional steel and wooden structures. The lodge was built up around the trees. There is a deck on the top of the building that provides an excellent view of the surrounding game reserve. On this observation deck is a placard marking the spot where Queen Elizabeth took the English throne. She was visiting Treetops when her father, the King George VI died in 1952, and she became "Queen" Elizabeth.

There are not large numbers of animals in this game reserve, but we did see our first, and only, rhinoceros. There has been a lot of poaching of rhinoceros. Africans kill these animals: and cut off the horn, which is highly valued as an aphrodisiac in Eastern countries. Consequently, rhinos are a rare sight.

The evening meal is a "family style" affair. Down the

middle of each table is a miniature train track upon which small railroad flatcars carry dishes of food past the diners.

After dinner we went to a lounge and watched animals through large glass windows. It gets cold at night in Nairobi, and animal watching is done inside. There are floodlights around a pond area that has been "seeded" with food to attract nocturnal creatures.

Treetops is a four-star restaurant. It's expensive, and doesn't require a lot of physical stamina. Consequently, it caters to older tourists who are not concerned about prices. There are better game lodges for tourists with children. One of these is Kilaguni Lodge at Mount Kilimanjaro. That was the next stop on our Christmas vacation.

From Treetops we traveled south through Nairobi and then another two hours to Tsavo National Park and Kilaguni Lodge. Mount Kilimanjaro is just a short distance west of Kilaguni. This provides a spectacular view of Mount Kilimanjaro, especially at sunrise. This is one of the nicest areas in East Africa. It's amazing to see Mount Kilimanjaro rising up from the semi-desert landscape with its snow-capped peaks. I say "peaks" as there are two. The African safari driver said that the more famous peak that is most commonly seen is considered "male" and the shorter peak is the "female." The Kilaguni Lodge provides safari drivers to drive tourists around Tsavo National Park. We had the VW, so we simply drove around taking pictures of the animals. We parked under trees and took pictures of the lions in the branches overhead. We were also chased by an elephant who had a calf and thought we were getting too close. Now, that's "thrilling." She, the "mama" elephant, only chased our car for a short distance. Just far enough to let us think we were in real trouble.

After driving through the park most of the afternoon, we had dinner in the lounge. As in Treetops, the area next to the lounge is lit by floodlights and "baited" to attract animals. Here, however, since it's much warmer than Treetops, there were no glass windows. There is a knee-high brick wall separating the lounge area from the animal feeding ground. I don't know why the animals don't come leaping through the lounge, but they didn't the night we were there.

The guests stay in small cabins located in a semi-circle around the main lounge/dining room. These cabins look like a cement version of native huts. Very nice. You may request early morning tea. An African waiter arrives at the cabin about 6 a.m. with a pot of hot tea and some biscuits. Each cabin has a porch area that looks out on Mount Kilimanjaro. It was "fantastic" to drink tea, eat biscuits, and watch the sun rise on Mount Kilimanjaro. That must be the best that it gets in East Africa. Great!

The trip to Treetops and Kilaguni Lodge was going to be hard to beat, but we were expecting the Lodge at Murchinson Falls on the Nile to be good also. We were not disappointed.

This was our last vacation time before going home, so we wanted to pack everything into it we could. We returned to Tororo from Treetops and Kilaguni, spent a week at home answering mail, taking care of household chores, and were off to the northwestern part of Uganda to Para Lodge in Murchinson Falls National Park. The Nile River flows through this Park and Para Lodge has luxury tents built on wooden floors just next to the main lodge. This was much the same arrangement as the cabins at Kilaguni, only these were tents. As we lay in our beds in the tent that night, we could hear the hippos along the Nile. During the day, the hippos stay in the water, with just their nose sticking out. During the evening, these huge animals come out of the water and forage the fields next to the river. Hippos make a sound like someone laughing—"YUUKKK, YUUKKK, YUUKKK,"—somewhat like huge pigs. "Hey, kids," I would say, "Here's a good joke for the hippos—a white horse fell in the mud!" Then from the river banks we would hear a chorus of "YUUKKK, YUUKKK, YUUKKK!" It sounded like the hippos were laughing at my joke about the white horse. Hippos are not the friendly, laughing pigs that they may seem when you hear them at night from a distance. If one is close to them when they are out of the water feeding in the evening, it can be dangerous. The *Uganda Argus* had this article about hippos:

MASAKA HIPPOS BIT VILLAGERS

Hippos in the Kitabule River, Kyotera County, Masaka have attacked villagers and bitten them.

In one incident, a man and his daughter were bitten at Minziro, in the Gombolola region of Kyebe, Kannabulemu, and were treated at Kyebe Dispensary. Later, Anamaria Nnamugera, the daughter of Mr. Yosefu Mukasa, was taken to Masaka Hospital with injuries which were found to be serious. Villagers at Minziro said the hippos had several times tried to attack people.

It has to be remembered that hippos are very large animals who take very "big bites." An African guide at Murchison Falls told us that his brother had been bitten "in two" by a hippo. Now, that's a "big bite."

The next day we had a boat ride on the Nile River from Para Lodge up to Murchison Falls—about 10 miles. We saw hippos, crocodiles, and monitor lizards in the water. There were elephants, giraffe, waterbuck, Cape buffalo, and all kinds of birds along the banks.

Now, we had done all the "tourist" things. It was time to concentrate on the last semester of school at TGS and plan our trip back to the States. It wouldn't be long now. I still didn't know if that was "good" or "bad."

26

The Vespa was ideal for the traveling that I did in and around Tororo. There were only two roads—east and west between Kampala and Nairobi, and north to Mbale. The Kampala to Nairobi road had little traffic, the road to Mbale had less.

I always took my camera along when I drove the Vespa. I never knew when some bizarre spectacle would unfold itself before my eyes. For example, in the Bigisu district of the Mbale road, I saw two women, running down the road, beating drums that were balanced on their heads. These two "drummers" were followed by several running and screaming women. Some of these women had their faces painted white, others held aloft ears of corn, or pangas. I pulled over, got out the camera, and starting taking pictures as these women ran past. I had no idea what was going on.

When the pictures were developed, I showed them to some Bigisu students at TGS. I hoped they would be able to tell me what had been going on. These Bigisu students looked at the pictures and laughed, saying, "Twins have been born! The women with white flour on their faces are relatives. The others are women from the village. When twins are born, we beat drums and scream to scare evil spirits away from the new-born twins. If this is not done, one of the twins will die."

On that same road one day, I saw an American

Twins have been born. People in village paint a white circle of flour paste around the face to scare the devil away so one baby will not die.

woman. As I approached, she flagged me down. I stopped, and she asked if I would give her a ride. She was going to Mbale. "What are you doing here?" I asked. "I'm in the Peace Corp, and I'm assigned to a project near Mbale. I'm coming back from the hospital. I go there every day for a shot." I knew of a small, Catholic first-aid station in that area. "What do you get a daily shot for?" I asked. "Well," she said, "I was bitten by a shrew, and I have to take a rabies shot. They give me a shot in the stomach every day for 15 days. In order to tell if the shrew was rabid, the head would have to be frozen and sent to England for tests. That couldn't be done, so I have to take the 'cure'—just to be safe." As we rode along to Mbale, I asked her about the quality of care she received in the first-aid clinic. She said that there was usually a Dutch nun who gave her the daily shot. "One day the Dutch nun was not there," she said, "and an African nurse asked me where I got the shot? I pointed to several different places on my stomach and said; sometimes here, sometimes here, sometimes here, and sometimes here." The African nurse filled the syringe and gave her a shot in each of the points the woman had indicated with her finger—four shots! She was supposed to get "one" shot a day, not four. "Why did you let her give you four shots?" I asked. "I was afraid to tell her what to do." She explained.

There were two other times I saw "Europeans" walking along the road in Tororo. Once, I met a woman from Australia. She claimed to be hitchhiking from England to South Africa. She had landed in London, and hitchhiked her way to Greece. From Greece, she "hitched" a ride on a boat to Port Said, Egypt. From that point, she had walked and hitchhiked south. I can't imagine that. A lot of "bad things, man" can happen between Egypt and South Africa.

Two Peace Corps men asked if they could pitch their tent in our yard. They were hitchhiking through East Africa and seemed to be having a "good time."

They recounted an experience when an elephant stuck his trunk inside their tent one night and "sniffed" The man who was telling me the story said, "I can laugh about it now; but that night, when I turned on my flashlight, and saw this big, grey, foul-smelling trunk "sniffing" us all over, I thought I would shit my pants."

Our British neighbors, Mr. and Mrs. Townsend, said that one night they heard a knock on the door and an American, male voice saying UEB." "UEB?" Mr. Townsend said to his wife, "Uganda Electric Board? Do we know any Americans working with the Uganda Electric Board?" They opened the door and saw an American with a python draped over his shoulders. "UEB—"the American said, "United Evangelical Brethren. We're missionaries from Congo on our way to Nairobi. My snake is hungry. Do you think there are any rats around these buildings he could catch? When he gets hungry, he gets mean."

The UEB's pitched their tent and spent an overnight. The next morning, they said that their "pet" snake must have caught some rats, because he seemed satisfied. Off they went to Nairobi. Now, these UEB missionaries stop at the Townsend's whenever they pass through Tororo.

I met a man and woman in a VW bug with Arizona license plates. "You just get in Africa?" I asked. They would not be able to use those Arizona license plates for more than a month after arriving in country. "Yes," he said, "Just got in this week." "Where are you working?" I asked. "Oh, no, we're not working here. We're just passing through." He went on to explain that he had taken a year off from teaching at Phoenix College. They had driven through Mexico, Central America, and South America. From Argentina they had put the VW on a boat and sailed to South Africa. From South Africa they were driving to Egypt, where they planned on taking a boat to Greece. From Greece they were going to drive that VW bug to England, get on another boat, sail to New York, and drive back to Phoenix. I took the their address and promised them a visit when I got back to the States. I paid them a visit in Glendale, Arizona, the year after I had returned to the States—brave souls!

You meet a lot of "unusual" people along the roads in East Africa. I was probably as "unusual" to these people as they were to me.

I ran out of gas on the Vespa between Mbale and Tororo. The Vespa had an emergency gas reserve, which gave me another 50 miles of fuel. When the motor died, I just had to "flip" a switch for another hour's driving.

The motor died, I "flipped" the switch, and found that I had already had my one "flip" sometime before—I had forgotten to fill the tank! The Vespa came to a stop, and I started pushing it along the road toward Tororo. Soon, there was a crowd of men, women, and children walking along with me. Everyone was having a "delightful time" talking, laughing, and yelling to others in the bush. It was like leading a parade down the road. Our parade went on for about a half hour, when a flatbed truck stopped. There were several African men sitting on the back of the truck. I asked them for a ride; they lifted both the Vespa and me on board, and we went on to Tororo.

Another time, I returned to Tororo from Jinja at night. I had gone to Jinja to purchase a part for our van at the VW garage. By the time I had gotten the part I needed, it was dark. There was no place to stay in Jinja, and I had to get home. I was afraid that something—animal or human—would step out of the darkness in front of the Vespa. That would have been a disaster! I stopped a big diesel truck at Owen Falls Dam and paid him to drive under 50 miles per hour home, so I could "tailgate" the truck back to Tororo. That was the worst hour's drive I ever had on that Vespa. By the time I got to Tororo, I was sick from the diesel fumes, but I was alive.

I never took a long trip on the Vespa again.

27

No one was in the classroom. The students were in their dorms packing their clothes, books, and personal items for the return to their villages. The room was so quiet. Occasionally, I could hear the voices of the TGS students calling to one another in the dorm area of the campus. I was feeling very sad. I would never see this place or these faces again.

My personal items were cleaned out of the room, but I checked everything one last time. The green chalkboard in the front of the room was filled with notes from my students. "Goodbye, Mr. Stewart." "We will always remember you and pray for you, Mr. Stewart." "Tell Paula and Beth we love them." "Tell John John and Stephen goodbye for us." There were dozens of these "best wishes." Reading them didn't make it any easier to leave.

I was about to walk out and lock the door when I saw a folded sheet of paper on my desk. It had "Mr. Stewart" neatly typed on the outside. I opened the folded sheet and read:

6th June, 1969
Dear Mr. Stewart,
    You know what? I feel so bad when I think of your leaving! When I think of it too much I find myself in tears. Do you think I'll ever get a teacher as good as you? NEVER. You are so good to us that every member of 4-c is very sad about your leaving.

You have been so good to us that we shall *always* and *ever* remember you. We have enjoyed all your jokes and stories you used to tell us. We have liked your teaching and we have liked you yourself as our teacher.

Mr. Stewart, I can't find the proper words to express myself but I guess you know how I and my fellow students feel about the whole thing. We shall miss you so much!

Yours faithfully,
Esther Kigundu

I walked outside and down the campus sidewalk to the front of the school where the Vespa was parked. As I walked along, I heard students calling from the buildings: "Goodbye, Mr. Stewart." I waved and called back, "Goodbye, good luck on the Cambridge." "We pray for you." a student called.

Why did I feel so sad about leaving Africa and going home to the States? I think it was because I was "wanted" and "needed" in Uganda. There are thousands who teach what I teach in the States—some are much better than I am, and some are much worse. I am average in the States—in Uganda I am "Bwana Kubwa."

I had enjoyed teaching and living in Tororo. No one will ever be like the Gatchells, or the Andrezejewskis, or Phyllis Roop, or Elwyn Doubleday. What a great group of people! I am proud to have been associated with them.

There were still a lot of things to do. First, we had to decide what we wanted to take home with us. We could sell and/or give away the rest.

The VW would be sold to the man who has the Volvo garage in Tororo. Volvo had an offer in *Newsweek*. If I purchased a Volvo and picked it up in Sweden, Volvo would license it for the summer to use in Europe and ship it to New York for me. The summer license and shipping to the States would be free.

The Vespa would also have to go. I wouldn't have much use for a motor scooter in Allegany County. One of the African staff at TGS wanted the Vespa.

The furniture and appliances would stay with the house. What did that leave to pack up and ship back? Not much—some books, clothing, shoes, photographs, and African souvenirs. Some things we would take with us—the ostrich egg. I would carry my ostrich egg in the camera bag. If that's broken, how would we replace it?

The packers came, and we sent the sea freight out. The VW was gone, the Vespa was gone, and we had only our personal luggage. It was just like it had been when we first arrived in Tororo two years before.

There was no one to say "goodbye" to. In June everyone was either leaving for the States or going on R&R. I remembered Bill Gatchell's poem about "Government." Bill had planned a trip to Norway to visit Ellen's relatives. They had to cancel that and fly on American carriers straight back to the States. However, I was willing to pay for parts of our return trip in order to make some stops on the way back. We didn't have a "strict" timetable for returning. I didn't have to start teaching at SUNY at Alfred until the last week in August. Our return trip gave us stops in Nairobi, Cairo, Athens, and Paris. At Paris we would put the children on PanAm and send them home. Joyce and I would then fly to Stockholm, where we would pick up our new Volvo and have a two-week Scandinavian summer vacation. We would then drop the Volvo off at the Volvo factory for shipment to New York. After which, we would fly back to the States.

We had decided to send the children back from Paris. They didn't want to travel in Europe again. They wanted to get back to the States and stay with their grandparents while Joyce and I spent two weeks in Denmark, Norway, and Sweden.

Pan Am said they would put the kids in the first-class section where they would be under the constant supervision of one of their attendants. My parents would pick them up at the Pan Am office at Kennedy Airport in the States. The first-class accommodations and supervising attendant for the kids would be at "no additional charge."

As the plane lifted off the runway at Entebbe, I looked out the window and watched the banana trees and African villages vanish from sight as we flew into the cloud cover—the last time I would ever see Uganda again. I thought I would feel sad, but I was over that now. I was excited about seeing Nairobi one last time. We made one last trip to Bazaar Street, the "quaint shops," and one last night at The Fair View. The next morning we were off to Egypt.

The air in Cairo felt like an "oven" as we stepped off the plane. There was strange lettering on signs. How do they ever read that, I wondered? We were standing in front of the customs counter with four children and several pieces of luggage.

"Today is my birthday!" said an Egyptian customs officer. "Well," I said, "Happy birthday to you, sir." "I thought you might want to help me celebrate my birthday," said the Egyptian with a smile on his face and a gleam in his eye. Here it comes, I thought. "What did you have in mind," I asked? "Each tourist entering Egypt can purchase two bottles of spirits from the duty-Free Shop," the Egyptian said. "You and your wife can purchase two bottles of scotch and two bottles of gin to help me celebrate my birthday. Of course, I will pay you for the purchase." "What if I don't want to celebrate your birthday," I asked? "That would be very unfortunate for you," said my

Egyptian friend. "I am afraid that we will have to inspect all your luggage very carefully. I am sure you have something in those bags that is not allowed in this country." "Well," I said, "Happy birthday. Let me help you celebrate." The Egyptian smiled and told the custom inspectors, "We won't have to look at this luggage, just load it in the airport shuttle for our friend." I purchased the specified scotch and gin and brought it to the van waiting outside the Duty-Free Shop. On the way to the hotel, I tried to compute the value of dollars and piasters to see if I was being "short changed" by our "Happy Birthday Boy." The amount he refunded me seemed to be correct. When we unloaded the van at the hotel, the four bottles of "booze" were gone. I don't know where those bottles went; but, they were not in the van when we reached the hotel.

Egypt's climate reminded me of Phoenix—hot and dry. That evening we were all sitting on folding chairs in the dark. I could see the stars overhead and feel the sand shift under my shoes. John was looking at the audience around us. We could hear quiet whispers in the crowd.

Suddenly floodlights came on and we saw the Sphinx. "I AM THE GUARDIAN OF THE NILE!" I recognized Richard Burton's voice. I looked at the children's faces in the reflection of the floodlights on the Sphinx. Their eyes were staring at the spectacle before us. The children "loved" it.

The light and sound show at the Sphinx was delightful. The Sphinx was awash in floodlights of various colors. Then the pyramids lit up—a history lesson in living color. I am glad we had the privilege of seeing this. We lucked out. The day prior to our arrival in Egypt this show was in German. The following day it would be in French. We were in the right place at the right time.

From atop a camel, I thought of Bernard Crix's advice as we were leaving Tororo—"Whatever you do, don't have your picture taken sitting on a camel," he had said. Bernard was a British teacher at Manjasi Boys School in Tororo. He will get a picture of our camel ride. "Oh, that's bloody tacky!" He will say. We didn't have much choice. We had climbed up the side of a pyramid—I didn't realize there were entrances into these things. We walked right down to the bottom of the pyramid into a large room that had held the coffin. I saw graffiti on the walls dated 1906. Andrew was here in 1906! There is a lot of graffiti inside this pyramid. "Abdul Ababa Gazondbah, 1936" The world is filled with graffiti. It's in subways, bathrooms, on bridges, schoolroom desks, stone cliffs, trees, monuments, buildings, and books. It's not a new thing. Even our cave-dwelling ancestors had graffiti on their walls.

We stepped out of the pyramid and were about to step down onto the sand, when "zap!" We were all being picked up by some Arabs and hoisted atop camels. The camera was slipped off my shoulder, and a white cloth was fastened on my head with a decorative rubber strap. I turned around and saw that each of the children and my wife were also atop camels. Click, click, click . . . the Arabs had "captured" this moment on the film in my camera. Now the world will know that we are "bloody tacky."

Shopping for souvenirs was great. All the shopkeepers were anxious to get American Express Traveler's Checks. They gave a better exchange rate than the Bank of Egypt. We bought camel saddles, pottery, and brass candlesticks. Bargain prices! After a day in the Museum of Antiquities and shopping, we had enough Egypt. Tomorrow we would be in Greece.

"I must see your money exchange chits," said the Egyptian customs woman who was processing our baggage and passports as we were leaving Cairo airport. "I don't understand what you want." I told this uniformed woman. "You claimed $2,000 American dollars in traveler's checks when you entered Egypt. Now, you have $1,500 in traveler's checks. You must show me bank chits for $500 American." "I don't have any chits," I said, "I just spent the traveler's checks when I bought things. I didn't go to a bank."

The customs woman called another woman over. I think this was her "supervisor" or someone she had to report to. They were talking and shaking their heads. Here I was again. In trouble at an airport in a foreign country. How do I get into these situations?

"It's against Egyptian Law," the Egyptian woman said, "to exchange money in any place other than the bank. You were told that when you came into the country. You have broken the law. This is very serious." Actually, the "Happy Birthday Egyptian" had gotten us through Egyptian customs so fast, that I was not "told" about the money exchange laws or anything else. "I am very sorry, but I'm sure you can help me with this," I said as I put my remaining Egyptian "piasters" into her hand. She didn't smile, but directed us to the proper gate for our flight to Athens. I was getting good at this sort of thing.

Athens was not as hot as Cairo. The people were starting to look more like me. The prices, however, were "out of this world." The camera I bought in Nairobi for $250 was priced at $1,200 here. I asked the desk clerk at the hotel why the prices were so high. He told me that it is because of the high government import duty.

There was a brochure in the hotel lobby advertising a one-day boat cruise in the islands. The kids all wanted to go, so we signed up. The next morning we got on a bus that took us to the docks.

It was a beautiful day, and the water was a clear,

blue color. There were three islands on this cruise. The first island was the Greek equivalent of "quaint shops." We walked through cobblestone streets buying Greek vases, and small decorative wool mats. There were no vehicles on this island.

The second island had beautiful sand beaches. We swam and relaxed on the beach. There was no shopping on this island, just sand beaches for swimming and sun bathing.

We had one last stop. This would be the island where we would have lunch. The boat tied up to a dock that was an extension of a nice restaurant. The floors of the restaurant were glass, allowing a nice view of the water below. The dining area was open and gave the feeling of being on a pier over the water.

After dinner, the boat started back to Athens. The boat reminded me of the Staten Island Ferry boats. There was an inner cabin with bus-like seats, a snack bar, and bathrooms. There was an observation deck on top with a railing around it.

Some of the people were relaxing in the main cabin and some were up on the observation deck. The wind picked up and the waves gave the boat a gentle "heaving" up and down. The people on the observation deck were enjoying this. The boat lifted up in the air, and came down—"OOOH, ... WEE!" "OOOH, ... WEE!" Everyone was holding on the rail, laughing and "OOOH, ... WEEing!" in enjoyment.

The wind picked up, and the waves got higher—"AAHH, ... UGH!" The people were getting sick. It was too rough to enjoy. People were leaning over the rail on the observation deck vomiting down the side of the ship. These were seas that only seasoned "salts" could enjoy.

There was a stairway leading to the observation deck. A woman dressed in an attractive, blue suit was going up the stairs. At the top of the stairway was a woman who was sick. She was vomiting into the wind. The blue-suited woman didn't see her at the top of the stairs. OOHHHYYYUUUKKK—the woman vomited at the top of the stairs. The brisk sea breeze caught the vomit half-way down the side of the boat and sprayed this "liquid" all over the woman in the blue suit. She looked "puzzled" as she wiped something wet off as the side of her face. Then she looked up the stairway and realized what she had been hit with. She turned, and started down the stairway—OOOHHHYYYUUUKKK—now she, too, was vomiting over the side of the boat.

The sun went down and the wind kept getting stronger. No one was up on the observation deck. People were sick all over the boat. The toilet in the men's room wouldn't flush and was brimming to the top with vomit. The sink was full of vomit, sloshing back and forth with the rocking action of the boat. The children were asleep. We gave them "seasick" pills after dinner and they became sleepy early. The boat was a mess, and I felt like I needed a shower. I had not gotten sick, but it took determination. I put my hands over my ears, looked down, and kept saying, "You will not be sick, You will not be sick, You will not be sick." Just like Dr. Kim's operating room. I think it would have been a lovely trip if the wind had not come up. It just got too rough for these "landlubbers."

When we got to Paris, the kids flew back to the States. This was a big event for our little town. In fact, it made the *The Sandy Creek News*.

STEWART CHILDREN COMING FROM PARIS

Greene Point—Mr. and Mrs. Paul Stewart are at the Point for two weeks vacation. On Sunday Mr. Stewart will fly to New York City to meet their four grandchildren who are flying in from Paris and will visit them for three weeks while their parents tour Europe, returning the end of August.

It's never over till the fat lady sings. She wasn't "singing" yet, but I could see something moving behind the curtains. We still had to pick up our new Volvo.

Joyce and I went on to Sweden and picked up the Volvo the next day. The rest of the time in Europe was spent between missing Tororo and missing the kids and the States. It was good to be finally going one place or the other.

When we stepped out of the plane in New York City everything looked the same as it had two years before. It was over. I was no longer "Bwana Kubwa." I was just another American returning from Europe.

28

We moved back to Alfred, and I resumed my teaching duties at SUNY at Alfred. Joyce was happy again. We had saved enough for a down payment on our own home. The children were happy with their new house, their new school, their new friends, and, yes, their new dog.

It wasn't the same for me, though. I missed the "excitement" of living in Africa. We didn't have the evenings with friends who had just returned from trips to exotic places. There were no discussions with Gatchell in which we solved the world's problems. No one called me "Bwana Kubwa," and I was not important to anyone. No one came to my home for GG shots, and I was not welcome in hospital operating rooms. We didn't talk with ambassadors or presidents of countries. No one was interested in my opinion on important issues. It was kind of dull. I even had to mow the lawn and wash the car. Onyango did that for me in Tororo.

I had been called "Bwana Kubwa" for two years in Uganda, and I guess I had started to believe it. Alfred brought me back to my true station in life—"Bill Stewart." Oh, well, fame and importance are fleeting. We still had the shortwave radio we had purchased in Uganda, and I listened to the BBC. However, it just wasn't the same, and, of course, the income was not the same. We had saved enough in two years in Uganda to pay cash for a new Volvo, have two trips to Europe, see the game parks of East Africa, and make a down payment on a house. It was hard for me to make this adjustment back to our SUNY at Alfred "living style."

The children told their teachers that we had slides of our two-year stay in Africa, and I was asked to visit their classes and show the pictures. The Stewart children loved this; especially when their pictures came on the screen in these African scenes.

I missed the climate of Uganda, the beauty of Uganda, the traveling, the diversity of culture, the feeling of making a contribution to society, and the exposure to different opinions.

To my wife, Joyce, Uganda had been like a two-year prison term with a total deprivation of friends and family. She rejected everything that was not as it had been in the States. To me, Uganda had been a breath of fresh air. It had been a time of growing and weighing of my own values. I felt more self-confident and open to the opinions of others. I could now say to myself, "Perhaps you are wrong about this," and make my own decisions without the bias of what I had been told by those around me. I could finally question, make my own decisions, and feel confident that my values were my own and not "learned" from others.

Uganda was two years full of personal growth and contribution. There were African girls who hadn't seen a typewriter before coming to my classes who were now going to take the place of British expatriates. These girls could type, take shorthand, and knew how businesses operated. I had done my job. These TGS students were going to help build a nation. I was proud of them.

I was proud of the letter that Esther Kigundu had placed on my desk the day I left Tororo. She could not have typed that letter two years before. She had been in my classes and had learned how to type a neat letter with proper punctuation, spelling, and placement on the page. That was my contribution to the people of Uganda.

Tororo Girls School was a good USAID project. I am sure that there were other worthwhile AID projects. To try to compose a list of AID'S accomplishments would never tell the complete story. Most of all, we were making African friends for the United States.

I remember having a conversation with an American tourist in Kampala. He asked me if I thought we were "doing something worthwhile" in Uganda. While we were talking, an African clergyman approached us and put his arms around me in the typical African-style greeting and said, "Mr. Stewart, I met you at Tororo Girls School. My daughter, Euleni, is your student. Thank you for coming to our country to help us." Perfect timing! The American tourist smiled and said, "Well, I guess this man has answered my question. Keep up the good work!"

"Tororo Girls" have taken positions in the Ugandan Ministry of Finance, Ministry of Agriculture, and Ministry of Tourism. Our students held jobs in banks, in resort hotels, and with airlines. One woman from Tororo Girls School went on to become the Minister of Education. There are also Tororo Girls in the foreign service of Uganda.

The two most personally enriching years of teaching I have ever had were spent at Tororo Girls School. I wouldn't have missed it for the world. Thank you Elwyn, Phyllis, Bill, George, and the TGS 4-c girls. Asanti sana. Kwahari, mami twani. (Thank you very much. Goodbye, don't die.)